S0-ABT-844

Thank You

for requesting "The original cookbook fundraising program."

This sample cookbook contains more features than any other cookbook of equal price on the market today. More options can be found at www.fundcraft.com.

Options featured in this Sample Book:
- Fundcraft soft cover design C1041 with plastic comb binding (blue)
- 4 free local information pages, table of contents and copyright page
- Local information pages and first section of book printed on designer Cross background paper
- 7 recipe sections featuring a different color divider set in each section
- Round tab option on Vegetable divider
- Heavy card stock option on Breads divider
- Different recipe format in each section to show print quality
- Continued and non-continued recipe feature in different sections
- Alphabetical and contributor index
- Merchant advertising can raise additional money
- Mail order page helps sell your cookbooks
- 16-page helpful hints section
- Recipe Notes
- Recipe Symbols
- Full-color photo on outside back cover FREE with order of 500 cookbooks

You can review all cookbook options at our website, www.fundcraft.com, or call one of our friendly customer service representatives.

1-800-853-1363

Features marked in red can be located in the Fundraising Guide and Catalog by referring to the corresponding page numbers.

Gracious Gifts

Designer Cross
Background Paper
(page 65)

Sponsored by

Bottom Lands
Community Church
Somerville, Tennessee

Rev. John Doe, Pastor

OFFICERS
and
COMMITTEE MEMBERS

President ....Jane Smith
Vice-President ....Wanda Doe
Secretary/Treasurer ....Stephanie Jacoby
Committee Chairman ....Jessica Perkins
Typing Personnel...Sandra St. John
                                                      Margaret Bell

A

Expression of Appreciation

Our organization, the compilers and sponsors of this cookbook, would like to thank and express our sincere appreciation to the many people in the community who gave so generously of their time and energy in collecting and submitting recipes and assisting with the sale of our cookbooks. Without their help, this book would not have been possible.

Bottom Lands Community Church
Somerville, Tennessee

Local Information Page using FREE Black & White photograph

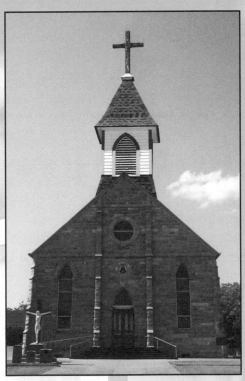

Bottom Lands Community Church

Somerville, Tennessee

Extends a Cordial Welcome to All Services

Sunday
- Morning Worship ....10:00 a.m.
- Children's Worship ....10:00 a.m.
- Evening Worship ....6:00 p.m.

Wednesday
- Choir Rehearsal ....6:00 p.m.
- Mid-Week Service ....7:00 p.m.

Rev. John Doe, Pastor

DEDICATION

We dedicate this book to all cooks. In our homes today, as always, life is centered around the kitchen. It is with this thought in mind that we, the sponsors, have compiled these recipes. Some of the recipes are treasured family keepsakes and some are new; however, they all reflect the love of good cooking.

Our thanks to all those who generously contributed their favorite recipes. Without their help, this book would never have been possible.

We hope you will enjoy the many outstanding and treasured recipes on the pages that follow.

Bottom Lands Community Church
Somerville, Tennessee

TABLE OF CONTENTS

FREE
Table of Contents

🕐   Quick & Easy

🌶   Hot & Spicy

FREE Recipe Symbols
(page 64)

Copyright © 2010
Fundcraft Publishing, Inc.

All rights reserved. Reproduction in whole or in
part without written permission is prohibited.

Printed in the U.S.A. by

P.O. Box 340 • Collierville, TN 38027
800-853-1373 • fundcraft.com
Specializing in church and school fundraising programs

Appetizers, Relishes & Pickles

This section highlights samples of:

- Full-Color Divider (Set D88)
- Helpful Hints Divider Back
- Recipe Format F6
- Cross Background Paper
- Church & Crosses Graphics
- Non-Continued Recipes
- Christian Art Fillers

Divider Set D88 - CrossBlueSky (coordinates with Cover Design C1041)

Appetizers are treats that can be served either at the start of a meal or at a reception or open house. Listed below are suggestions for quick and easy appetizers, along with some advice to follow for staying within the guidelines for a healthy diet:

Salsa has become one of America's most popular foods, primarily from its abundant use as an appetizer. Not only is salsa tasty, but it contains little or no fat.

For a change from basic salsa, mix with an equal amount of refried beans and top with cheese. Heat in the microwave and serve hot.

Chips are the natural companion to salsa, including potato chips and corn chips. Most potato and corn chips are fried, and therefore, contain a high level of fat. Baked chips, or even baked pretzels, are a good alternative when used with salsa. The taste of the salsa generally makes up for any loss of taste from baked rather than fried chips.

Cut, raw vegetables arranged on a tray can make a decorative and colorful appetizer. Salad dressings make easy vegetable dips, but try to use low-fat versions. Most regular salad dressings are loaded with fat. Low-fat sour cream can be mixed with ketchup and garlic powder to make an easy vegetable dip.

Cream cheese has long been a versatile food to build a quick appetizer around. Reduced fat cream cheeses are a good choice. Top cream cheese with any of the following for a quick and easy appetizer:

- green pepper jelly
- drained small shrimp and cocktail sauce
- chopped pickle or pickle relish
- a dash of worcestershire sauce and chives
- chopped chutney and a dash of curry powder

Each of these combinations can be served with crackers, thin-sliced toast or chips.

Copyright © 1996 by Fundcraft Publishing, Inc.

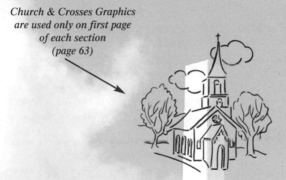

Church & Crosses Graphics
are used only on first page
of each section
(page 63)

Recipe Format 6
(pages 62-63)

APPETIZERS, RELISHES & PICKLES

ROASTED RED PEPPER APPETIZERS

4 large red bell peppers,
remove tops, cut in half
and seed
2 c. Ricotta cheese
2 eggs

½ tsp. salt
¼ c. chopped basil
½ c. grated Parmesan cheese
olive oil

In a 350° oven, place peppers, skin side up, on a broiling pan and roast peppers until skin is black. Cool in a brown paper bag. Then peel off skin.

In a medium bowl, mix Ricotta cheese with eggs, salt, basil and cheese. Put in a cupcake pan or 4 small ramekins, about ½ cup each; brush with olive oil.

Take roasted peppers and line each pan, leaving an overhang of pepper. Fill the center with the Ricotta cheese mix. Cover with the overhanging pepper and bake for 30 minutes in a 350° oven.

If you are using ramekins, place on a cookie sheet for easier handling. Each serving should look like an upside-down cupcake. After cooling for 5 minutes, take a butter knife and run over sides of pan; place a dish over it and remove. Serve warm with Italian bread over a green salad for garnish.

Sue Jones

MEXICAN CHEESE CAKE

1 lb. cream cheese, softened
2 c. (8 oz.) shredded Cheddar
cheese
2 c. sour cream, divided
1 ½ pkg. taco seasoning mix

3 eggs (room temperature)
1 (4 oz.) can green chiles,
drained and chopped
⅔ c. salsa

Preheat oven to 350°. In large bowl, combine cheese. Beat until fluffy. Stir in 1 cup sour cream and taco seasoning. Beat in eggs, one at a time, mixing well after each. Fold in chiles.

Pour into 9-inch spring-form pan. Bake 35 to 40 minutes or until center is firm. Remove from oven. Cool 10 minutes. Spoon remaining 1 cup sour cream over cheese cake. Bake 5 minutes longer. Cool completely.

Cover and refrigerate several hours. Before serving, remove sides of spring-form pan and top with salsa. Serve with plain taco chips.

Kathy Coats

CRISPY CHEESE WAFERS

8 oz. sharp cheese
1 stick margarine
1 c. flour

½ tsp. salt
1 tsp. red pepper
1 c. Rice Krispies

Grate cheese and cream with margarine. Sift dry ingredients and add to the cheese mixture. Fold in Rice Krispies. Let stand in refrigerator overnight.

Roll into balls and flatten with a fork. Bake on an ungreased cookie sheet for 12 minutes. Makes about 5 dozen.

Pam Moore

*Non-Continued Recipes
using Christian Art Fillers
(page 64)*

ITALIAN CHEESE BALL

4 (3 oz.) cream cheese,
  softened
⅓ c. grated Parmesan cheese
¼ c. mayonnaise

½ tsp. oregano
⅛ tsp. garlic powder
parsley flakes

Combine all ingredients. Chill slightly and form into a ball. Before serving, roll ball in parsley flakes, chopped nuts or leave plain. Serve with bread sticks or crackers.

Angie Smith

FREE Recipe Symbols
(page 64)

BALSAMIC TOMATOES

leaf lettuce
Roma tomatoes
olive oil

balsamic vinegar
tomato basil Feta cheese
fresh basil

Line serving plate with lettuce. Slice tomatoes and place on top of lettuce. Mix 2 parts olive oil with one part balsamic vinegar. Shake or whisk to blend thoroughly. Pour over tomatoes. Top with crumbled tomato basil Feta cheese. Garnish with chopped fresh basil.

This recipe can be made in any quantity you wish. It is good served on Triscuits, bagel chips or toasted French bread. Any leftovers are great on top of a salad for lunch the next day.

Note: *This recipe was given to me by my friend Sue Wilson.*

Elizabeth Clark

Recipe Notes
(page 64)

HOT BROCCOLI DIP

½ large onion, chopped
½ stick butter
3 (10 oz.) pkg. chopped
  broccoli

2 cans cream of chicken
  soup
1 (6 oz.) pkg. Rondelle
  semi-soft garlic cheese
3 oz. mushrooms, sliced

Saute onion in butter. Cook broccoli. Put broccoli, onion, soup, cheese and mushrooms in large pan and heat until bubbly. Serve with dip-size corn chips.

Micky Diaz

HAM ROLL-UPS

18 oz. cream cheese
2 cans deviled ham
1 bunch green onion,
  chopped

1 small can crushed
  pineapple, drained
2 tsp. honey
8 large flour tortillas

Mix all together and spread on tortilla. Close up ends of tortilla to keep spread from falling out. Refrigerate for several hours, then slice into bite-size pieces.

Martha Hewitt

SWEET SPICED NUTS
(Makes 2 cups)

Bold Ingredient Listing Format 6

1 c. hazelnuts
½ tsp. cinnamon
¼ tsp. salt
1 Tbsp. lightly beaten egg
  white

½ c. sugar
¼ tsp. allspice
1 c. whole blanched almonds

Preheat oven to 350°. Put oven rack in the middle position. Toast hazelnuts in a large, shallow pan until golden and skins are blistered (10 to 15 minutes). Wrap nuts in a kitchen towel and let steam 1 to 2 minutes, then rub off any loose skin. (Don't worry if all the skins do not come off.) Cool completely.

Reduce oven temperature to 325° and line a shallow baking pan with parchment paper. Mix the sugar and spices in a large bowl. Whisk egg white in a bowl until foamy; add the hazelnuts and almonds. Toss to coat. Transfer nuts to the sugar mixture and toss to coat. Arrange nuts in one layer in the pan and bake (shaking pan occasionally) for 20 to 25 minutes or until the nuts are golden brown.

Cool nuts completely in pan on a rack. Will keep for 2 weeks in an airtight container.

Jeanne Andreano

Bold Contributor Name Format 6

ARTICHOKE DIP
(Makes 2 Cups)

½ c. grated Parmesan cheese
1 c. mayonnaise
1 garlic clove, minced

1 can artichoke hearts,
drained

Preheat oven to 350°. Cut artichoke hearts into small pieces and combine all ingredients. Bake until bubbly. Serve with crackers.

Suzy Baldwin

LACQUERED PECANS
(Makes 2 Cups)

2 c. pecans, lightly toasted
½ c. brown sugar, firmly
   packed
⅓ c. balsamic vinegar

½ tsp. kosher salt
¼ tsp. chili powder or
   cayenne pepper (optional)

Line a cookie sheet with parchment paper. Combine pecans, brown sugar and vinegar in a large frying pan. Over medium-high heat, cook, stirring constantly, until the sugar has melted and the pecans are coated with the mixture. There should be no liquid at the bottom of the pan.

Transfer pecans to the prepared sheet, separating nuts with a fork. Cool.

Marilyn Powell

COCKTAIL NIBBLERS
(Makes 8 Cups)

½ stick butter
½ c. brown sugar
½ c. white Karo syrup
1 box Quaker Oat Squares
1 c. chopped pecans

1 tsp. baking soda
1 tsp. vanilla
handful of pretzel sticks
(optional)

Preheat oven to 250°. In a large pot, boil butter, sugar and syrup. Remove from the heat and add baking soda and vanilla; it will foam. Mix squares and pecans into mixture. Spray a baking sheet with nonstick spray and spread mixture on baking sheet. Bake for 1 hour, stirring every 20 minutes. Remove from the oven and let cool for 15 minutes. Break into pieces and store in a covered container.

Chris Iulo

REDHOT BUFFALO CHICKEN DIP
(Makes 5 Cups)

8 oz. cream cheese
½ c. Blue cheese or Ranch
salad dressing
½ c. Frank's RedHot Buffalo
wing sauce

½ c. crumbled Blue cheese
or shredded Mozzarella
cheese
2 c. shredded cooked
chicken (optional)

Preheat oven to 350°. Place cream cheese in a deep-dish 9-inch plate; microwave 1 minute to soften. Whisk in salad dressing, hot sauce and cheese until smooth. Stir in chicken. Bake 20 minutes or until heated through and stir. Garnish as desired. Serve with crackers or vegetables.

Microwave Directions: Prepare as above; microwave, uncovered, on High for 5 minutes or until hot, stirring halfway through cooking.

Tip: For a party buffet table, keep this dish hot in a small crock-pot or fondue pot.

Loretta Cutrer

HOT CRAB DIP
(Serves 6 to 8)

1 c. fresh lump crabmeat
8 oz. low-fat cream cheese
⅓ c. mayonnaise
2 tsp. lemon juice
1 Tbsp. water
2 green onions, sliced

3 Tbsp. chopped parsley
1 Tbsp. horseradish
½ tsp. Tabasco
¼ tsp. Worcestershire sauce
½ c. slivered almonds
  (optional)

Preheat oven to 350°. Beat together cream cheese, mayonnaise, lemon juice, water, onions, parsley, horseradish, Tabasco and Worcestershire sauce until smooth. Fold in crabmeat. Pour into a baking dish and top with almonds. Bake for 30 minutes or until bubbly. Serve with bread rounds or pita chips.

Barbara Smith

ARTICHOKE AND SPINACH DIP
(Makes 2 Cups)

10 oz. pkg. frozen chopped
  spinach, thawed and
  drained
27 oz. (2 cans) artichoke
  hearts, drained and
  mashed

¾ c. mayonnaise
¾ c. sour cream
1 ½ c. grated Parmesan
  cheese
salt and pepper to taste
bagel chips

Preheat oven to 350°. Drain all water from spinach. Mix all ingredients (except chips) together. Bake in a greased casserole dish for 30 to 40 minutes. Serve with bagel chips.

Anita Loeser

BLACK BEAN SALSA
(Makes 4 Cups)

1 can black beans, drained
and rinsed
1 jar medium hot salsa (Pace
or Ortega)

3 green onions, chopped
1 tsp. cumin or to taste
1 Tbsp. chopped cilantro
1 avocado

Combine all ingredients except avocado. Gently mix. Peel and cut avocado into medium-sized chunks. Fold into salsa. Serve with your favorite tortilla chips.

Note: *I usually double this recipe; it is a crowd pleaser. Enjoy!*

Recipe Notes

Nancy Clay

BRANDIED CHEESE DIP
(Serves 10 to 12)

7 oz. Gouda or Edam cheese,
grated
8 oz. pkg. cream cheese

1 c. sour cream
3 Tbsp. brandy

Preheat oven to 350°. Mix together all ingredients and bake for 30 minutes or until hot and bubbly. Serve with sliced apples and crackers.

Preserve color by dipping apples into lemon and water before serving.

Jean Koch

NEIMAN-MARCUS DIP
(Serves 12)

1 ½ c. shredded cheese
(Cheddar, Monterey Jack
or mixed)
2.5 oz. sliced almonds
¾ c. cut up scallions (with
greens)

½ jar Hormel bacon bits
1 c. sliced water chestnuts,
drained and chopped
1 c. mayonnaise
crackers

Mix all ingredients together. Let sit for 1 to 2 hours. Serve with crackers.

Note: *I use 5 to 6 slices of turkey bacon, cooked crispy, instead of the bacon bits. I have never served this spread without being asked for the recipe!*

Brenda Rounds

CHEESE DIP

8 oz. cream cheese, softened
¾ c. mayonnaise
8 oz. shredded Swiss cheese
½ pouch bacon pieces
(usually found in the salad
dressing section)

2 to 3 green onions or
scallions (chop greens
only)
1 box Ritz crackers or Ritz
chips

Preheat oven to 350°. Combine first 5 ingredients (cheese through scallions). Put into a casserole dish. (I use a quiche pan.) Bake for 15 minutes; remove from the oven and crumble some crackers on top. Bake for an additional 5 minutes. Serve with crackers.

BLACK BEAN DIP

15 oz. can black beans,
  drained and rinsed
1 Tbsp. chopped jalapeno
  pepper
¼ c. finely chopped onions
¼ c. sour cream

½ tsp. salt
2 Tbsp. picante sauce
1 ¼ c. grated Cheddar
  cheese
tortilla chips

Preheat oven to 350°. Mash beans with a fork (leaving some chunks). Add jalapeno pepper, onions, sour cream, salt, picante sauce and 1 cup of cheese; mix well. Pour into a 1-quart baking dish and sprinkle with remaining cheese. This may be refrigerated at this point. Bake 20 to 30 minutes. Serve with tortilla chips.

Joyce Kopenhaver

BLACK BEAN SALSA
(Makes 3 cups)

15 oz. can black beans,
  drained and rinsed
1 c. finely chopped Roma
  tomatoes
½ c. fresh or frozen corn
  kernels, blanched
4 green onions, sliced ¼-inch

2 Tbsp. chopped cilantro
2 Tbsp. freshly squeezed
  orange juice
½ tsp. green Habanero chili
  or Louisiana hot sauce
¼ tsp. ground cumin
⅛ tsp. salt

Combine all ingredients, being careful that there is not too much liquid. Serve with tortilla chips or in baked wonton skin cups. Buy the small rectangular skins and bake them in the mini muffin tins until crisp. You can trim off the corners to make them rounder if you have time. Do not get them too brown. Cool and fill with drained salsa.

Susan Kampfer

STUFFED MUSHROOMS

20 to 30 large mushroom
  caps
1 stick melted butter
1 ½ c. crabmeat, flaked
2 large eggs
3 Tbsp. mayonnaise

2 tsp. lemon juice
1 c. Stove Top stuffing,
  prepared
2 Tbsp. melted butter
2 c. six-cheese Italian
  shredded cheese

Dip mushroom caps in melted butter. Place in a baking dish. Mix the crabmeat, eggs, mayonnaise, lemon juice, butter, Stove Top suffing and 1 cup of cheese. Fill the caps with mixture. Bake at 375° for about 15 to 20 minutes. Larger size caps will take longer. Top with remaining 1 cup of cheese and bake for another 5 minutes or until cheese melts.

Julie Sharp

NACHOS

1 lb. ground beef
½ pkg. taco seasoning
sliced cheddar or Jack
  cheese

sliced jalapeno
round tortilla chips

Crumble ground beef in skillet and brown, making sure to break up the pieces. Add taco seasoning and water and cook until mixture is reduced and mixture sticks together.

Place tortilla chips on cookie sheet or pizza pan. Layer a spoonfull of meat mixture, cheese and jalapeno slice on each chip. Bake in 400° oven until cheese melts. Serve immediately.

Optional: Garnish with avocado dip and sour cream.

Susan Smith

DEVILED BISCUITS

1 pkg. canned biscuits
¼ c. butter or margarine

1 (4 ½ oz.) can deviled ham
¼ c. grated Parmesan cheese

Snip biscuits in quarters. Arrange in 2 (8-inch) round baking dishes. Heat butter and deviled hame together, stirring until blended. Pour hot ham mixture over biscuit pieces, being sure to coat each one well. Sprinkle with Parmesan cheese.

Bake in hot oven at 400° about 15 minutes or until golden brown; serve hot. Makes 40.

Beverly Faust

ROLLUPS

8 large flour tortillas
1 (8 oz.) pkg. cream cheese
1 (8 oz.) pkg. sour cream
16 slices turkey breast
  sandwich meat
1 (7 oz.) pkg. fresh spinach
  leaves, rinsed well and
  drained

1 (4 oz.) pkg. alfalfa sprouts,
  rinsed and dried
2 large tomatoes, seeded and
  chopped
8 oz. Havarti cheese sliced

Spread each tortilla with 1 ounce cream cheese, then 1 tablespoon sour cream. Arrange 2 turkey slices atop each, then didide spinach leaves, alfalfa sprouts, tomatoes and cheese evenly over turkey. Roll up each filled tortilla tightly from one side to the orther securing with toothpicks. Chill. At serving time, cut crosswise into slices for tasty, wheel-shaped sandwiches.

Jane Pulse

SHRIMP DIP

1 (8 oz.) pkg. cream cheese, softened
¾ c. mayonnaise
3 Tbsp. Catsup
Juice of one lemon

1 lb. cooked shrimp drained
1 stalk celery (finely chopped)
1 medium onion grated (optional)

Combine cream cheese, mayo, catsup & lemon juice. Blend until smooth. Stir remaining ingredients. Cover and refrigerate overnight. Serve with crackers or chips. Yields about 4 cups.

Melanie Stoll

CHEESE BALL

2 (8 oz.) cream cheese (softened)
3 to 5 small stalks green onions chopped
⅓ jar Hormel bacon bits

½ pkg. original ranch dressing
black pepper & salt to taste
chopped pecans

Mix first four ingredients and add black pepper & salt. Mix well with larges spoon. Shape into ball and roll in chopped pecans. Chill overnight. It is better if it sets overnight. You may want to double this recipe for a large cheese ball. I serve with wheat thins.

Dianne Barber

CHEESE KRISPS

2 c. grated Cheddar sharp cheese
2 sticks oleo, room temperature

2 c. flour (plain)
2 c. Rice Krispies
¼ - ½ tsp. red pepper (1 use ¼)

Beat butter, cheese, flour, then add Rice Krispies and red pepper and blend. Do not grease cookie sheet. ½ tsp. Put on cookie sheet, pierce with wet fork, bake 10 minutes at 325°.

Dianne Barber

BEAN DIP

2 cans bean dip
2 avocados or Kraft avocado
  dip
1 pkg. taco seasoning

1 Tbsp. lemon juice
6 Tbsp. mayonnaise
4 Tbsp. sour cream

Mix avocado and lemon juice together. Mix taco seasoning, mayonnaise and sour cream together then layer bean dip, avocado and lemon juice, and sour cream, top with cheese diced tomatoes (onions and black olives optional)

Melanie Stoll

DRIED BEEF CHEESE BALL

3 pkg. (8 oz.) cream cheese
1 bunch green onions,
  chopped
1 small can chopped ripe
  olives (optional)

1 can mushrooms (optional)
1 jar dried beef, chopped
3 tsp. Accent
salt and pepper to taste
1 dash of Tony's seasoning

Mix all together and form into ball or divide into two balls. Serve with wheat thins.

Dianne Barber

SHRIMP DIP

2 (8 oz.) cream cheese
2 Tbsp. mayonnaise
1 bunch green onion
  chopped fine
1 celery stalk chopped fine

2 cans shrimp (pieces are
  good)
dash of Worcestershire
dash of Tony Seasoning

Mix together and refrigerate. (overnight is better)

Dianne Barber

APPETIZERS, RELISHES & PICKLES

CRAB MEAT SANDWICHES

1 c. mayonnaise
1 c. grated American cheese
¼ c. chopped green onions
1 can crabmeat, drained

1 or more pkgs. of hoagie
buns sliced thin for
sandwiches

Mix first 4 ingredients and spread thin over sliced bread. Toast on a cookie sheet in oven or in a toaster-broiler until brown. Serve hot.

Dianne Barber

MEAT BALLS

2 lbs. ground beef (chuck)
½ c. bread crumbs (dry
seasoned)
2 eggs, beaten

pinch of garlic salt
1 small chopped onion
1 or 2 Tbsp. of milk
salt and pepper to taste

Sauce:
2 bottles of chili sauce

1 medium or large jar grape
jelly.

Mix meat, onion, garlic salt, bread crumbs, and rest of ingredients. Shape into small balls; brown in skillet. Keep warm until ready to use. Combine chili sauce, and jelly. Heat sauce to simmer. Add meatballs. Cook in crock pot at low heat for 2 to 4 hours.

Dianne Barber

MINI PIZZA SQUARES

baked whole wheat snack
crackers
salsa (smoked)

pepperoni, diced
Mozzarella cheese, shredded

Place crackers on cookie sheet. Put a spoon of salsa on each cracker. Put small amount of diced pepperoni on top of salsa and top with shredded Mozzarella cheese. Place under broiler until cheese melts.

Peggy Ducan

PICKLED EGGS

12 to 16 hard boiled eggs
2 c. white vinegar
2 Tbsp. sugar
1 tsp. salt
1 to 2 tsp. pickling spice
1 medium onion, sliced

Combine ingredients and simmer for 5 minutes. Place eggs in jars. Cover with liquid. Put lids on jars and refrigerate overnight.

Margaret Jones

HOMEMADE PIMENTO AND CHEESE

1 (8 oz.) cream cheese
2 c. sharp Cheddar cheese
1 large jar diced pimento
½ c. mayo
salt and pepper to taste

Combine first four ingredients; mix well. Add salt and pepper to taste.

Sheryl Baker

Soups
Salads and Sauces

This section highlights samples of:
- **Full-Color Divider (Set D70)**
- **Helpful Hints Divider Back**
- **Recipe Format F6**
- **Family Gathering Graphics**
- **Continued Recipes**
- **Recipe Notes & Symbols**

Divider Set D70 - Bountiful Harvest (coordinates with Cover Designs C131 and C134)

*Each Fundcraft Full-Color Divider Set includes seven coordinating designs.
They are not made to mix and match between sets as seen in this sample book.

# Salads

Salads can be a good source of vitamins, minerals, and fiber. Follow these suggestions when including salads as a part of your family's well-balanced diet:

- Iceberg lettuce has few nutrients. Substitute a variety of types of lettuce such as raddichio, Boston, and Romaine.
- Avocados and olives are high in fat. Use these sparingly in salads.
- Cheeses also add fat to salads.
- Season salads with herbs instead of salt.
- Use low-fat or no fat dressings; limit other dressings to 1 tablespoon.
- Substitute yogurt for sour cream in homemade dressings.
- Substitute low-fat or no fat mayonnaise when making potato salad.
- Pickles and olives are high in salt. Use sparingly.

Additions and Garnishes
Sliced Hard-Cooked Eggs - remove
   yolks, which are high in cholesterol
Pimento
Radishes
Green Pepper
Chicken
Carrots
Celery
Tomatoes
Cooked Beets
Cauliflower
Broccoli

Tips For Tossed Salads
Wash greens, drain and dry well
   prior to storing.
Tear greens instead of cutting to
   avoid bruising with a knife.
Remove the waxy outer skin of
   cucumbers before slicing.
Marinate tomato wedges
   separately in a vinaigrette;
   then add to salad.
To core lettuce, smack head
   down hard on counter top.
   Then twist core out.

- Remember to use low-fat or fat-free crackers as an accompaniment to salads!
- Check the labels on soups for ingredients you wish to avoid. Many commercially prepared soups are very high in salt and fat.
- When preparing homemade soups, use margarine instead of butter and herbs instead of salt.
- Many recipes call for milk as an ingredient for soups and sauces. Use skim milk or 1% if possible.
- When preparing dressings, use vegetable oils such as olive, sunflower or canola. These contain less fat and as with all vegetable oils ... they contain *no cholesterol!*

Copyright © 1996 Fundcraft Publishing, Inc.

Family Gathering Graphics

✦✦✦

SOUPS, SALADS & SAUCES

FREE Recipe Symbols   Recipe Format 6

♥

CHICKEN MINESTRONE

1 pkg. (3 to 4) boneless, skinless chicken breasts, cooked and cut into cubes
1 red onion, chopped
2 carrots, peeled and sliced
2 celery stalks
2 Tbsp. olive oil
2 cloves garlic, minced
3 c. chopped kale leaves
1 c. dry red wine

1 large tomato, seeded and chopped
4 c. chicken stock or broth
1 bay leaf
1 can cannellini (whole kidney beans)
¼ chopped fresh basil
salt and pepper
red pepper flakes
grated Parmesan cheese

Heat oil in a Dutch oven over medium heat. Add onion, carrots and celery. Cook, uncovered, stirring often, until softened, about 7 minutes. Stir in the garlic and cook for 1 minute. Add the kale and cook until wilted (about 2 minutes). Add the wine and tomato and bring to a boil. Reduce the heat to medium low. Cover partially and simmer until well-flavored, about 1 hour.

Add chicken cubes. Drain the beans. Rinse with cold running water and drain again. Add to the pot along with the basil. Season with salt, pepper and red pepper flakes. Simmer 10 minutes.

Recipe Notes

scard the bay leaf and ladle into warm bowls. Serve ...un grated Parmesan cheese.

Note: *To tell if a chicken is completely cooked, pierce it with a fork. If the juices run clear, it's done. If the juices are slightly pink, it needs to cook for another 5 to 10 minutes.*

Elizabeth Wilson

EASY CLAM CHOWDER

4 cans cream of potato soup
1 can cream of celery soup
1 soup can water
1 stick butter
3 cans minced clams

1 bunch green onions,
  chopped (tops, too)
1 (16 oz.) carton sour cream
pepper to taste

Saute green onions in butter. Add soups and water slowly. Heat. Add sour cream. Add clams and juice. Heat to a boil. Reduce heat. Let simmer 10 minutes, stirring constantly. (Do not boil.)

Suzanne Davis

FREE Recipe Symbols

CUCUMBER SALAD

2 cucumbers
1 can mandarin orange
  slices (undrained)

2 containers plain yogurt

Peel cucumbers and cut off ends (about ½-inch). Cut in half lengthwise. Cut cucumber halves into small slices and put into bowl. Add undrained mandarin orange slices and yogurt. Stir together. Refrigerate and serve as side dish.

Janie Rider

CREAM OF CILANTRO SOUP

1 bunch fresh cilantro
1 (32 oz.) pkg.
  reduced-sodium fat-free
  chicken broth, divided
2 Tbsp. butter
2 Tbsp. all-purpose flour
1 (8 oz.) pkg. fat-free cream
  cheese

1 (8 oz.) container light sour
  cream
1 garlic clove, minced
¼ tsp. salt
¼ tsp. ground red pepper
¼ tsp. ground cumin

Garnishes:

fresh cilantro sprigs

light sour cream

Recipes continue to next page

Remove stems from cilantro and coarsely chop leaves. Process cilantro and 1 cup chicken broth in a blender or food processor until blended, stopping to scrape down sides.

Melt butter in a Dutch oven over medium heat; whisk in flour. Gradually add remaining 3 cups broth, whisking constantly, until mixture is smooth. Boil 1 minute. Stir in cilantro mixture, cream cheese and next 5 ingredients. Simmer soup 15 minutes. Garnish, if desired. Yields 6 cups. Prep Time: 5 minutes. Cook Time: 20 minutes.

Beth Meadows

Recipe continued from previous page.

TOSTADA SALAD

1 lb. ground beef	1 c. chopped onions
1 envelope taco seasoning	¼ tsp. salt
1 head romaine, cut in	2 c. grated Cheddar cheese
pieces	6 tomatoes, cut in wedges
2 avocados, sliced	1 c. French dressing
1 (15 oz.) can red kidney	1 (9 oz.) pkg. taco chips
beans, drained	

Brown beef with onions; drain. Add beans, seasoning mix and salt.

In salad bowl, combine remaining ingredients, reserving 1 cup chips. Add beef mixture to salad bowl and toss lightly. Garnish with reserved chips.

Bold Contributor Name Format 6 **Betty Jeffries**

POTATO SOUP

5 medium potatoes, diced	1 Tbsp. dried parsley flakes
1 small onion, chopped	2 cubes chicken bouillon
1 stalk celery, chopped	4 c. water
2 tsp. celery salt	4 slices bacon
1 tsp. seasoned salt	2 Tbsp. flour
1 tsp. dried whole basil	1 ½ c. milk
¼ tsp. pepper	

Combine first 10 ingredients in large Dutch oven. Bring to a boil. Cover and reduce heat. Simmer 20 minutes.

Cook bacon in large skillet until crisp. Remove bacon, reserving 3 tablespoons drippings in skillet. Crumble bacon and set aside.

Add flour to drippings in skillet; stir until smooth. Cook 1 minute, stirring constantly. Gradually add milk; cook over medium heat, stirring constantly, until thick and bubbly.

Gradually stir milk mixture and bacon into potato mixture. Simmer, uncovered, 15 minutes. Yields 2 quarts.

Amelia Rose

FREE Recipe Symbol

HOMEMADE PICANTE SAUCE

1 qt. fresh stewed tomatoes
6 green onions
1 Tbsp. garlic powder

1 c. jalapeno peppers
¼ c. salt

Drop tomatoes into boiling water; boil for 1 minute. Drop in cold water; skin and core. Put in food processor. Chop finely, then bring to boil; mash. Add ¼ cup salt and simmer with lid for 10 minutes.

Process remaining ingredients in food processor. Remove seeds from jalapenos first. Add all other ingredients to tomato mixture. Boil for 10 minutes, stirring continuously. Chill and serve.

Mary Sue Helms

Recipe Title & Ingredients printed in bold, easy-to-read type

ITALIAN VEGETABLE SOUP

1 lb. lean ground beef
1 c. onion, chopped
1 c. celery, sliced
1 c. carrots, sliced
2 cloves garlic, minced
16 oz. can tomatoes
15 oz. can tomato sauce
15 oz. can red kidney beans, drained
2 c. water
3 tsp. beef bouillon granules

1 Tbsp. dried parsley flakes
1 tsp. salt
½ tsp. oregano
½ tsp. sweet basil, chopped
¼ tsp. black pepper
2 c. cabbage, shredded
1 c. green beans (fresh or frozen), cut into 1-inch pieces
½ c. small elbow macaroni

Brown beef in large heavy kettle. Drain off fat and add all ingredients, except cabbage, green beans and macaroni. Bring to a boil. Lower heat, cover and simmer for 20 minutes. Add cabbage, green beans and macaroni; bring back to a boil and simmer until vegetables are tender. If you prefer a thinner soup, add water to broth. Sprinkle with Parmesan cheese before serving.

Dorris Bowman

CORN AND BLACK BEAN SALAD

15 oz. can whole kernel corn, drained
15 oz. can black beans, drained and rinsed
1 red bell pepper, finely chopped

½ c. green onions, diagonally sliced
½ c. red onion, chopped
1 clove garlic, minced
1 medium tomato, chopped
1 jalapeno pepper, seeded and finely chopped

Dressing:
¾ c. Italian salad dressing
¾ tsp. hot pepper sauce
½ tsp. chili powder

1 Tbsp. fresh lemon or lime juice
1 Tbsp. fresh cilantro, chopped

In a large bowl, combine corn, beans, bell pepper, green onions, red onion, garlic, tomato and jalapeno pepper. Mix dressing ingredients and put into a jar with tight-fitting lid; shake well. Pour over corn mixture and stir until all mixed. Refrigerate, covered, at least 6 hours or overnight.

Nancy Klesert

KENTUCKY CORNBREAD SALAD

4 to 5 cornbread muffins, crumbled
1 ½ c. fresh tomatoes (about 6 Roma), diced
½ c. sweet onion, diced
½ c. green pepper, diced

1 lb. bacon, cooked and crumbled
¼ c. sweet pickle relish
¾ c. mayonnaise
¼ c. sweet pickle juice
Parmesan cheese, shredded

Place crumbled cornbread in large salad bowl. Combine tomatoes, onion, green pepper, bacon and relish. Add to cornbread crumbs. Combine mayonnaise and pickle juice; mix well. Pour over vegetables and cornbread; toss gently. Sprinkle with cheese. Chill until ready to serve. Serves 6 to 8.

Linda Elder

CHILI

2 lb. ground beef
1 large onion, chopped
1 Tbsp. garlic, minced
1 large can crushed tomatoes
2 cans diced tomatoes with green chilies

2 cans chili beans
1 envelope dry chili mix
2 cans water
chili powder to your taste (if needed)

Brown hamburger with onions and garlic; drain off excess fat. Combine rest of ingredients and simmer for 1 hour. Adjust taste temperature to your likeness with chili powder or hot peppers. Serve with shredded cheese and corn chips.

Kim Myers

WHITE CHICKEN CHILI

4 chicken breasts
(boneless/skinless)
48 oz. jar Great Northern
beans

24 oz. jar salsa (medium)
10 oz. can chicken broth
8 oz. Monterey Jack cheese,
shredded

Cut chicken into 1-inch pieces. In a crock-pot or stove top pot, place raw chicken, Northern beans, salsa and chicken broth; mix well. Cook over low heat for 1 ½ hours on stove top or 2 to 3 hours in crock-pot. Add grated cheese and serve when completely melted. Garnish with fresh cilantro, avocados and sour cream, if desired.

Kathy Clark

HOT CHICKEN SALAD

2 c. chicken, cooked and
diced
½ c. slivered almonds
2 Tbsp. lemon juice
1 c. Cheddar cheese,
shredded

1 c. potato chips, crushed
1 ½ c. celery, diced
2 Tbsp. onion, chopped
¾ c. Miracle Whip salad
dressing

Mix together all ingredients, except potato chips. Put into a greased 2-quart casserole dish. Top with potato chips and bake in 375° oven for 30 minutes. Serves 4.

Beth Aitken

RED KIDNEY BEAN SALAD

15.5 oz. can dark red kidney
beans
¾ c. celery, chopped
½ c. small red onion,
chopped fine

2 hard-boiled eggs, chopped
fine
4 Tbsp. no-fat mayonnaise
1 tsp. lemon juice

Mix mayonnaise and lemon juice. Pour into rest of ingredients. It's better if it sits awhile in refrigerator for a couple of hours.

Marlene Ailes

POTATO SOUP WITH SHRIMP

¼ c. butter
1 small onion, diced
2 medium carrots, diced
2 Tbsp. flour
8 medium Russet potatoes,
    peeled and cubed
4 c. milk
2 chicken bouillon cubes,
    dissolved in ½ c. hot milk

1 c. half and half
1 tsp. salt
¼ tsp. pepper
1 lb. medium shrimp (raw)
crumbled bacon bits (for
    garnish)
grated sharp Cheddar
    cheese (for garnish)

In 4-quart saucepan, melt the butter and sauté onion and carrots until both are slightly tender, about 5 minutes. Whisk in the flour and cook for 1 minute. Add the potatoes, milk and dissolved bouillon cubes. Cook over medium heat for 15 minutes, until the potatoes are very soft and some of them have begun to dissolve into mush. Add the half and half, salt and pepper. Let cool, then refrigerate until serving.

In a small saucepan, bring 2 cups slightly salted water to a boil. Add the shrimp all at once and stir well. Watch the shrimp closely; as soon as they turn pink, turn off the heat and drain. The shrimp should be slightly undercooked. When they are cool, peel them and chop roughly into big chunks and place them in a plastic bag. Refrigerate until serving.

Reheat the soup over very low heat (it will stick to the bottom of the pot if you heat it too quickly), about 45 minutes before serving. When the soup is hot, add the shrimp and stir well. Garnish with bacon bits and cheese when serving.

Bella Dekker

HOMEMADE MINESTRONE SOUP

2 cloves garlic, minced
3 large ribs celery, diced
4 to 5 small carrots, diced
½ large sweet onion,
chopped
4 slices pancetta
1 can Del Monte Italian style
stewed tomatoes

1 can dark red kidney beans,
drained and rinsed
1 can cannellini beans,
drained and rinsed
20 oz. can beef broth
1 bunch fresh rosemary,
chopped
salt and pepper to taste

In large pot on high heat, fry pancetta until browned. Add onion next. After a minute, add celery, carrots and garlic. Reduce to medium heat. Cover and cook 10 minutes. Add kidney and cannellini beans that have been drained. Add entire can of tomatoes, beef broth, salt, pepper and fresh rosemary. Cover and simmer slowly ½ hour.

Dawn Jones

CAULIFLOWER SALAD

½ medium head lettuce,
shredded
1 head cauliflower, broken
into small pieces
1 c. mayonnaise or Miracle
Whip
1 Tbsp. sugar

1 small onion, sliced and
separated
½ lb. bacon, fried and
crumbled
4 oz. Cheddar cheese,
shredded

Mix sugar into mayonnaise and set aside. Layer lettuce, cauliflower and onions into a 9 x 13-inch glass dish. Spread dressing on top; sprinkle with bacon and cheese. Cover and refrigerate overnight.

Georgia Oldenberg

MARINATED CABBAGE

1 head cabbage, shredded
1 large onion, sliced

several carrots, shredded
(optional)

Dressing:

1 c. vinegar
1 large onion

2 c. sugar

Prepare cabbage mixture and set aside. Bring dressing ingredients to a boil and pour over cabbage. Cover and let stand for 24 hours.

Julane George

RAMEN NOODLE SALAD

2 pkg Ramen Oriental
noodles, broken up (save
seasoning)
1 lb. broccoli slaw mix

1 c. sunflower seeds
1 c. pecan pieces
1 bunch green onions, thinly
sliced (optional)

Dressing:

½ c. vegetable oil
½ c. sugar
⅓ c. red wine vinegar

2 seasoning packets from
Ramen noodles

Mix all salad ingredients together and toss well. Make dressing and pour over salad at least 15 minutes prior to serving. Mix well.

Cande Vermeulen

SPINACH SALAD

6 to 10 oz. pkg. spinach,
shredded or baby leaves
4 to 8 oz. mushrooms, sliced
2 green onions, chopped

almonds
bacon bits
mandarine orange segments

Dressing:

1 c. sugar
1 c. oil
½ c. vinegar
1 tsp. salt (optional)

1 tsp. paprika
1 tsp. onion powder or onion
juice
1 tsp. celery seed

Whip all salad dressing ingredients together until it thickens. Let stand at least 1 hour, shaking often. Toss all salad ingredients together in a large serving bowl then add dressing just before serving.

Laverne Swinehart

TACO SOUP

2 (15 oz.) cans tomatoes
(undrained)
2 (15 ½ oz.) cans sweet corn
(undrained)
1 pkg. taco seasoning
1 box Spanish rice
1 medium onion, finely
chopped
3 c. water

2 lb. ground sirloin or
ground deer
2 (15 oz.) cans chili beans
(undrained)
Baked Scoops
fat-free shredded Cheddar
cheese, grated
fat-free sour cream
(optional)

In large saucepan or Dutch oven, boil meat in enough water to cover; drain and rinse. Combine all ingredients except Scoops, cheese and sour cream. Bring to a boil. Reduce heat and simmer 5 to 10 minutes. Place Scoops in bowl; top with cheese. Add sour cream, if desired.

STUFFED PEPPER SOUP

2 lb. ground beef
1 (28 oz.) can tomatoes
1 (28 oz.) can tomato sauce
2 c. cooked rice
2 c. green pepper, chopped

2 beef bouillon cubes
¼ c. packed brown sugar
2 tsp. salt
1 tsp. pepper

In an 8-quart Dutch oven, brown beef; drain off fat. Add remaining ingredients; bring to a boil. Reduce heat, cover and simmer for 30 to 45 minutes or until peppers are tender.

POTATO SOUP

6 or 8 potatoes, peeled and
diced
1 onion, chopped
1 celery stalk, cut up
1 tsp. salt

½ tsp. pepper
1 qt. fat-free half and half
2 (14 oz.) cans fat-free less
sodium chicken broth
1 (14 oz.) broth can of water

Cook potatoes in chicken broth and water until almost done, then add onion, celery, salt and pepper. Add 1 quart of half and half; heat until hot. You may add instant potatoes to thicken. Serve with fat-free shredded mild Cheddar cheese on top.

SOUPS, SALADS & SAUCES

POTATO SALAD

6 or 8 potatoes, peeled and
  diced
1 small onion, diced
¼ c. mustard (more if
  needed)

4 to 6 eggs, boiled
3 Tbsp. mayonnaise
½ c. sugar to taste
½ c. sweet salad cubes
¼ tsp. salt

Cook potatoes 10 to 12 minutes. Boil eggs 10 to 15 minutes. Mix pickles, onion, mayonnaise, mustard, salt and sugar; let stand while potatoes and eggs are boiling. Drain potatoes and add to mixture. Peel eggs and dice into the potato mixture. Mix well.

INSTANT FRUIT SALAD

2 (14 ½ oz.) cans no sugar
  added fruit cocktail
1 (20 oz.) can chunk
  pineapple in pineapple
  juice

1 can mandarin oranges
1 small box sugar-free
  instant vanilla pudding

Drain juice from cocktail, pineapple and oranges. Add instant pudding to ingredients. Use some of the juice needed to dissolve pudding. Let set several hours in refrigerator.

PISTACHIO SALAD

1 (16 oz.) can crushed
  pineapple (undrained)
1 (3 ½ oz.) pkg. pistachio
  pudding

1 large Cool Whip
½ c. cottage cheese
½ c. nuts, chopped
1 c. miniature marshmallows

Dissolve pudding in pineapple; mix. Add remaining ingredients; mix well. Chill until set.

PISTACHIO SALAD (LITE)

1 (16 oz.) can crushed
  pineapple in pineapple
  juice (undrained)
1 (3 ½ oz.) pkg. sugar-free
  pistachio pudding

1 large fat-free Cool Whip
½ c. fat-free cottage cheese
½ c. nuts, chopped (optional)
1 c. miniature marshmallows

Dissolve pudding in pineapple; mix. Add remaining ingredients; mix well. Chill until set.

MACARONI SALAD

2 c. macaroni
1 tsp. salt
1 medium green pepper, chopped
1 medium cucumber, diced
1 medium onion, chopped
1 large tomato, diced
2 Tbsp. light or fat-free margarine

1 tsp. flour
1 c. Splenda or any sugar substitute
Egg Beaters equivalent to 1 egg
¼ c. vinegar
1 c. reduced-fat or fat-free mayonnaise

Cook macaroni according to package directions. Mix sugar substitute and flour. Mix together Egg Beaters and vinegar. Cook with butter and flour mixture until thickened. Remove from heat and add mayonnaise. Place cooked macaroni in colander; rinse and drain well. Mix with all other ingredients, then add dressing. Chill.

BROCCOLI SALAD

1 bunch broccoli (use only bud ends)
1 small purple onion

1 c. shredded Cheddar cheese
½ lb. fried bacon, crumbled

Dressing:

¼ c. sugar
1 Tbsp. vinegar

½ c. mayonnaise

Mix the ingredients together. Prepare dressing. Pour dressing over salad and mix well.

CAULIFLOWER AND BROCCOLI SALAD

1 large head cauliflower, cut into small pieces
1 large bunch broccoli, cut into small pieces

1 medium red onion, cut into small pieces

Dressing:

1 c. reduced-fat or fat-free mayonnaise
¼ c. olive oil
⅓ c. vinegar

½ c. Splenda or any sugar substitute
salt and pepper to taste

Cut cauliflower, broccoli and onion into small pieces. Mix together mayonnaise, oil, vinegar, Splenda, salt and pepper. Pour dressing over cauliflower mixture. Mix well.

SIX CUP SALAD

1 c. Cool Whip
1 c. crushed pineapple
1 c. miniature marshmallows

1 c. fruit cocktail
1 c. coconut
1 (8 oz.) pkg. cream cheese

Put cream cheese in bowl first. Drain pineapple and fruit cocktail. Stir in remaining ingredients. Chill and serve.

CHICKEN SALAD

3 c. diced cooked chicken
1 ½ c. diced celery
2 Tbsp. lemon juice
1 ½ c. seedless grapes, sliced

¾ c. toasted sliced almonds
½ tsp. salt
1 Tbsp. grated onion
2 hard-boiled eggs, chopped

Dressing:

1 c. mayo
¼ c. evaporated milk

salt and pepper to taste

Pour dressing over chicken mixture; mix and chill.

Shirley Cole Johnson

GRANDMA HELEN'S HOT CHICKEN SALAD

4 c. diced cooked chicken or turkey
2 cans cream of chicken soup
1 can cream of mushroom soup
6 sliced hard-boiled eggs
1 c. mayonnaise

2 c. celery, diced
1 medium onion, diced
1 Tbsp. lemon juice
salt/pepper
1 c. blanched diced almonds
3 c. crushed potato chips
1 c. grated American cheese

Combine all the ingredients, except chips and cheese. Put in a 9 x 13 (3-quart) casserole dish in layers with the eggs. Cover with the chips and sprinkle with the cheese. Bake at 425° for 20 to 30 minutes. Serve with a gelatin salad and hot rolls.

Sarah Siebert

PASTA CHICKEN SALAD

1 lb. fettuccine, cooked and drained
1 ½ c. Italian dressing
6 chicken breasts, cooked and cut in bite size pieces
1 (6 oz.) can sliced black olives
1 c. green onions, chopped
8 Tbsp. parsley
2 c. mayonnaise*
2 tsp. oregano
chopped walnuts

Mix fettuccine and Italian dressing and marinate overnight. Mix remaining ingredients night before. Next day, mix pasta and chicken salad by hand.

*Note: I use ½ lite mayo and ½ reduced-fat sour cream.

Sibby Lewis

GREEK PASTA SALAD

(With Shrimp, Tomatoes, Zucchini, Peppers and Feta)

Dijon Vinaigrette:

¼ c. rice wine vinegar
2 Tbsp. Dijon mustard
1 large garlic clove, minced
big pinch of salt
black pepper to taste
⅔ c. extra-virgin olive oil

Pasta Salad:

2 medium zucchini, thinly sliced lengthwise
1 medium yellow pepper, halved lengthwise and seeded
2 Tbsp. olive oil
ground black pepper and salt to taste
2 Tbsp. salt (for pasta water)
1 lb. medium pasta shells
1 lb. cooked shrimp, halved lengthwise
8 oz. (1 ½ c.) cherry tomatoes, halved
¾ c. coarsely chopped pitted Kalamata olives
1 c. crumbled Feta cheese
½ small red onion, cut into small dices
2 tsp. dried oregano

To make the vinaigrette, whisk together the first five ingredients, then slowly whisk in the oil for a thick consistency. Pour into a jar with a tight-fitting lid to transport it to the picnic.

Adjust oven rack to highest positio: *Recipes continue to next page* iler on high. Toss zucchini and bell pepper wi lt and pepper and arrange on a large baking sheet with sides. Broil eight to 10 minutes, until spotty brown, turning zucchini slices and pepper halves once. Set aside in a large bowl to cool, then cut into bite-sized pieces.

Bring 1 gallon of water and 2 tablespoons of salt to boil. Add pasta; boil, using package times, until just tender. Drain thoroughly (do not rinse) and dump onto the baking sheet. Set aside to cool.

Put vegetables, pasta and remaining ingredients (except dressing) in the bowl or a gallon-sized zipper bag (can be refrigerated for several hours). To serve, add dressing; toss to coat.

Sibby Lewis

Recipe continued from previous page.

TOSTADA SALAD

1 lb. ground lean beef	1 c. chopped onions
1 envelope taco seasoning	¼ tsp. salt
1 head romaine, cut in	2 c. grated Cheddar cheese
pieces	6 tomatoes, cut in wedges
2 avocados, sliced	1 c. French dressing
1 (15 oz.) can red kidney	1 (9 oz.) pkg. taco chips
beans, drained	

Brown beef and drain, after cooking with onions. Add beans, seasoning mix and salt. In salad bowl, combine remaining ingredients, reserving 1 cup chips. Add beef mixture to salad bowl and toss lightly. Garnish with reserved chips.

Betty Jeffreys

SMOKED SALMON AND AVOCADO

1 (8 oz.) pkg. smoked salmon,	3 ripe avocados, cubed
chopped	croutons, crushed slightly
kosher salt	½ lemon, juiced
fresh ground pepper	prepared Wasabi
prepared champagne	fresh chives, chopped (for
vinaigrette	garnish)

You will also need a 3-inch ring mold (biscuit cutter or tuna can ring).

In a small bowl, combine salmon and ⅓ cup champagne vinaigrette (more if desired) and salt and pepper to taste. Set aside. In another small bowl, place avocado and sprinkle with lemon juice to avoid discoloration. Add a little Wasabi and gently toss. Add more for a hotter taste.

Place the ring in the center of individual serving plates. Layer 2 to 3 pieces of salmon in the mold. Gently press down with the back of a spoon. Place 3 to 4 slices of the avocado on top of the salmon. Gently press down. Repeat the layers 1 more time. Remove the ring mold and garnish the top with small pieces of chopped chives. Repeat with remaining salmon and avocado. Makes 4 molds.

Valarie Wing

SHRIMP REMOULADE

½ c. olive or salad oil
½ c. tarragon vinegar
½ c. sliced green onions
½ c. horseradish mustard

2 Tbsp. ketchup
1 Tbsp. paprika
1 tsp. salt
2 cloves garlic, minced

In a screwtop jar, combine all ingredients; cover and shake well. Chill at least 4 hours. Pour on top of boiled shrimp on bed of shredded lettuce.

Kelly Davis

BAYLEY'S WEST INDIES SALAD

1 lb. fresh crab meat
1 medium onion, chopped
  fine
4 oz. Wesson oil

3 oz. cider vinegar
4 oz. ice water
salt and pepper

Divide chopped onion in half and spread ½ over bottom of large bowl. Separate crab meat lumps and place on top of onion, then spread balance of onion on top of this. Salt and pepper. Pour oil, vinegar and water over. Cover tightly.

Place in refrigerator to marinate 2 to 12 hours. When ready to serve, toss lightly. Do not substitute ingredients.

Meats
& MAIN DISHES

This section highlights samples of:
- Full-Color Divider (Set D71)
- Helpful Hints Divider Back
- Recipe Format F7
- Music Graphics
- Continued Recipes
- Recipe Notes & Symbols

Divider Set D71 - Simple Pleasures (coordinates with Southern Comfort Cover Design C154)

*Each Fundcraft Full-Color Divider Set includes seven coordinating designs.
They are not made to mix and match between sets as seen in this sample book.

Meat Cooking Chart

Roasting	Weight	Minutes Per lb.	Oven Temp.	Internal Temp.
FRESH PORK				
Rib and loin	3-7 lb.	30-40	325 F	175 F
Leg	5 lb.	25-30	325 F	170 F
Picnic shoulder	5-10 lb.	40	325 F	175 F
Shoulder, butt	3-10 lb.	40-50	325 F	170 F
Boned and rolled				
Shoulder	3-6 lb.	60	325 F	170 F
BEEF				
Standing ribs - rare	3-7 lb.	25	325 F	135 F
- medium	3-7 lb.	30	325 F	165 F
- well done	3-7 lb.	35	325 F	170 F
For rolled and boned roasts, increase cooking time 5 to 12 minutes.				
LAMB				
Shoulder- well done	4-10 lb.	40	325 F	190 F
Shoulder - boned and rolled	3-6 lb.	40	325 F	182 F
Leg- medium	5-10 lb.	40	325 F	175 F
Leg - well done	3-6 lb.	40-50	325 F	182 F
Crown - well done	3-6 lb.	40-50	325 F	182 F
SMOKED PORK				
Shoulder and picnic hams	5 lb.	30-40	325 F	170 F
	8 lb.	30-40	325 F	175 F
Boneless butt	2 lb.	40	325 F	180 F
	4 lb.	25	325 F	170 F
Ham	12-20 lb.	16-18	325 F	170 F
	Under 10 lb.	20	325 F	175 F
	Half Hams	25	325 F	170 F
VEAL				
Loin	4-6 lb.	35	325 F	175 F
Leg	5-10 lb.	35	325 F	175 F
Boneless shoulder	4-10 lb.	45	325 F	175 F
POULTRY				
Chicken	3-5 lb.	40	325 F	170 F
Stuffed	over 5 lb.	30	325 F	170 F
Turkey	8-10 lb.	20	325 F	175 F
	18-20 lb.	14	325 F	175 F
Duck	5-10 lb.	30	325 F	175 F

Copyright © 1996 Fundcraft Publishing, Inc.

Music Graphics

Meats & Main Dishes

Bacon Cheese Ring

Recipe Format 7
Recipe Title offset to left
Donor name offset to right

Beverly Taylor

3 c. Cheddar cheese	½ c. Mozzarella cheese
½ c. heavy mayo	1 c. cream cheese, softened
½ c. bacon bits	½ c. green onions, chopped
16 oz. strawberry preserves	¼ c. chopped pecans

In a bowl, mix shredded Cheddar and Mozzarella cheese. Add chopped green onions for color and bacon bits. Mix in softened cream cheese and mayo to firm up or it may not hold its form.

In a Tiara pan or pie dish, either coat with nonstick spray or lay a sheet of Saran Wrap. Sprinkle edges with pecan pieces and put cheese mixture into pan. Flip onto serving dish and top with strawberry preserves. Serve with butter crackers.

Note: *This makes a wonderful addition to a buffet table. Very colorful as well as delicious.*

Continued recipe feature
Recipes continue from
page to page

Salmon Mousse

Millie Wilkinson

(Servings: 12)

1 (15 oz.) can Pillar rock salmon	½ c. onion, chopped
2 envelopes unflavored gelatin	½ c. celery, chopped
¼ c. lemon juice	½ tsp. dill weed, dried
½ c. cucumber, peeled, seeded and chopped	½ tsp. salt
	1 c. mayonnaise
	1 c. whipping cream

Drain salmon, reserving liquid. Add water to salmon liquid to make 1 cup. Combine salmon liquid and gelatin in a small saucepan. Heat over medium heat until gelatin is dissolved, stirring constantly. Remove from heat and set aside. Remove skin and bones from salmon. Flake with a fork.

Place half of the liquid and half of the salmon with half of each of the next 8 ingredients in a processor or blender. Mix until smooth. Put this ture in a large container and repeat with the next h-'r ~edients. Add this to the previous batch. Stir all tog

Recipe continued from previous page.

Tι..υ mixture is now a liquid! Lightly oil the large mold or individual molds. Gently pour in the ingredients and refrigerate until firm.

Serve on a lettuce leaf and garnish with unpeeled cucumber rounds and lemon slices with crackers of choice on the side.

Crown Roast Of Pork With Rosemary

Joe Johnson

7 to 8 lb. crown of pork
  (about 12 chops)
¼ c. dry white wine
3 Tbsp. packed light brown
  sugar
3 Tbsp. olive oil

½ c. Dijon mustard
2 Tbsp. chopped fresh
  rosemary
2 large garlic cloves, chopped
salt and pepper to taste
¾ c. heavy cream

Set roast on a flat rack in a large roasting pan. In a bowl, mix together, wine, brown sugar, olive oil, mustard, rosemary and garlic. Brush this on roast, coating sides. Save remaining marinade in a small saucepan. Cover roast with plastic wrap and let stand at room temperature for 1 hour.

Preheat oven to 400°. Remove plastic wrap and scrape excess marinade off roast; add to saucepan. Season roast with salt and pepper. Roast 30 minutes. Reduce heat to 350°; roast until thermometer inserted into thickest part of meat registers 140°. For medium, roast about 1 ½ hours more.

Transfer roast to carving board; cover loosely with foil and let rest 20 minutes. Place saucepan with reserved marinade over medium heat. Add cream and boil sauce until reduced slightly, about 5 minutes. Season with salt and pepper. Serve pork chops with side of sauce.

Shrimp In Garlic Sauce

Anne Wilson

1 lb. large shrimp, peeled and
deveined
1 egg white
¼ c. cornstarch

1 to 2 Tbsp. water
2 c. vegetable oil
1 Tbsp. cornstarch, mixed
with 3 Tbsp. water

Sauce:

¼ c. chicken broth
¼ c. apple cider vinegar
¼ c. ketchup
3 Tbsp. black soy sauce
2 Tbsp. dry sherry

8 garlic cloves, crushed and
minced
2 Tbsp. finely minced ginger
5 Tbsp. sugar
1 tsp. chili paste (optional)

Butterfly the shrimp and rinse and drain well. Place the shrimp in a medium bowl and add the egg white, ¼ cup cornstarch and 1 to 2 tablespoons water. Mix well. The consistency should be silky and the color milky.

In a large pan or wok, heat the oil to 280°. Add the shrimp. Turn the shrimp gently. When they are white and fluffy, remove them to a colander and drain. Place on a serving dish.

In a small saucepan, mix the chicken broth, vinegar, ketchup, soy sauce, sherry, garlic, ginger, sugar and optional chili paste. Stir well. Bring the garlic sauce to a boil. Lower the heat to simmer for 5 minutes. Stir in the cornstarch mixture and bring to a boil, stirring until thickened. Pour sauce over shrimp and gently toss and serve.

Lasagne

Joan Hartley

Sauce:

1 lb. sirloin ground meat
1 lb. sausage, minus casing
1 small onion, chopped
2 (28 oz.) cans tomato puree

1 can water
1 Tbsp. sugar
1 Tbsp. salt
2 Tbsp. olive oil

In a large pot, brown the meat. Drain and set aside.

In the same pot, heat the olive oil; add onion and cook to a golden brown. Add puree, salt and sugar; stir for 3 minutes. Rinse the puree cans with water and gradually add to sauce. (Make sure it is only one can of water.) Add meat and simmer for 1 ½ hours. This sauce can be prepared a day or two in advance.

1 lb. lasagne noodles, follow
   pkg. directions
1 Tbsp. olive oil
3 lb. Ricotta
2 eggs, beaten

¼ c. chopped parsley
1 ½ c. grated Parmesan or
   Romano cheese
1 lb. shredded Mozzarella
   cheese

Cook noodles per package directions. Add oil to water (this makes the noodles easier to handle). Do not overcook. Drain and rinse with cold water. Drain again and set aside.

In a medium bowl, combine the Ricotta, parsley, cheese and eggs; mix well. On a clean and roomy surface, line up your pasta, sauce, Ricotta mixture, grated cheese and Mozzarella.

In a 9 x 13 casserole dish, pour ½ cup tomato sauce. Place a layer of lasagna noodles, spread some Ricotta mixture all over the top and top with sauce. Sprinkle on grated cheese and Mozzarella. Repeat this process until all ingredients are used.

Before baking, take a fork and go around the sides to make sure the sauce drips between the pasta and the casserole dish. Cover with foil. Bake in a 350° oven for 40 to 45 minutes. After lasagna has cooked, remove foil and let it settle for 10 minutes.

In Loving Memory of my grandmother, Mary Cunningham.

Italian Beef In The Crock-Pot

Sandy Dugan

4 to 5 lb. roast, cut up in
   small squares
2 to 3 beef bouillon cubes

1 tsp. garlic salt
2 Tbsp. Italian dressing
garlic bread or French bread

Place roast, bouillon cubes, garlic salt and Italian dressing in crock-pot. Add enough water to cover beef. Cook on low for 8 hours. Heat up garlic bread or spread garlic spread on French bread. Wrap in foil and heat in oven for about 10 minutes. Shred beef with fork and knife; serve with gravy on garlic bread. Add a salad and a vegetable to this "delicious" sandwich.

Salmon With Moroccan Salsa

(Serves 6)

6 fillets center-cut salmon
½ c. olive oil
¼ c. balsamic vinegar
1 Tbsp. chopped garlic
1 Tbsp. Worcestershire sauce
salt and pepper to taste
3 medium red and green bell
  peppers
1 Tbsp. olive oil
2 tsp. ground cumin

½ tsp. ground cinnamon
4 Tbsp. olive oil
½ c. kalamata olives
½ c. chopped red onion
⅓ c. chopped cilantro
¼ c. golden raisins
3 Tbsp. lemon juice
3 Tbsp. chopped mint
2 tsp. grated orange peel
½ tsp. cayenne (optional)

In a glass baking dish, mix ½ cup oil, vinegar, garlic and Worcestershire sauce. Season salmon with salt and pepper. Place in glass dish and spoon marinade over the fillets. Refrigerate for 12 hours.

Char peppers over gas flame or under the broiler until blackened on all sides, turning frequently with tongs so all sides are blackened. Transfer to a paper bag and seal. Let stand for 30 minutes or until cooled. Peel, seed and coarsely chop the peppers.

Heat 1 tablespoon oil in a pan; add cumin and cinnamon. Stir until fragrant and pour over the peppers. Mix in next 8 ingredients and remaining oil. Season salsa with salt and freshly ground pepper. Refrigerate for 12 hours.

Heat grill and bring the salsa to room temperature. Grill salmon as desired and top with salsa. This is excellent for salmon, tuna or chicken.

Note: *This is a wonderful "Supper Club" dish.*

 *Recipe Notes*

Salmon With Dill Sauce

(Serves 6)

6 (6 oz.) salmon fillets
1 c. dry white wine
1 c. chicken broth
6 peppercorns
2 tsp. lemon juice

⅔ c. heavy cream
¼ c. dry white wine
lemon juice to taste
1 Tbsp. chopped fresh dill
1 Tbsp. chopped fresh parsley

Place salmon fillets skin side down in a hot, slightly oiled sauté pan. This will put a nice golden color to the fish. Before adding the poaching liquid, turn fillets over with skin side down.

In a bowl, combine 1 cup wine, broth, peppercorns and lemon juice. Pour over fish and poach for 6 to 7 minutes on each side. Make sure the liquid comes to a boil to cook off the alcohol. In a pot, cook cream, ¼ cup wine and lemon juice to desired thickness. Add dill and parsley.

This recipe goes great with wild rice and roasted asparagus.

Caribbean Pork Tenderloin

Charlotte J. Kensky

1 ½ to 2 lb. pork tenderloin	½ c. red currant jelly
4 Tbsp. orange juice	¼ c. Dijon mustard
1 ½ Tbsp. Caribbean Jerk seasoning	1 ½ Tbsp. orange juice or rum

Preheat oven to 400°. Brush pork with 4 tablespoons orange juice and sprinkle evenly with the Jerk seasoning. Place in a greased pan. Roast for about 30 minutes and let sit for about 10 minutes. Slice diagonally into ½-inch slices. Arrange on a platter.

In a small pan, whisk together jelly and mustard over low heat. Stir in the orange juice. (If using rum, remove from the heat before adding rum.) Drizzle over meat and serve. Serves 4.

Salmon Loaf

Barbara Smith

1 lb. can salmon	1 tsp. chopped onion
milk	(optional)
egg	¼ tsp. salt
1 ½ c. soft bread cubes	⅛ tsp. pepper
2 tsp. lemon juice	

Preheat oven to 350°. Drain liquid from salmon into a measuring cup. Add milk to make ¾ cup of liquid. Flake salmon, removing bones and skin. Blend in egg; stir in remaining ingredients. Spoon lightly into a greased loaf pan or 1-quart baking dish. Bake for 45 minutes. Serve with lemon wedges. Serves 4.

Chicken Tetrazzini

1 lb. spaghetti, broken in half
and cooked
1 can cream of mushroom
soup
1 can cream of chicken soup
1 soup can milk
1 soup can chicken broth
2 c. chicken or turkey meat,
cooked and diced
1 c. Cheddar cheese, shredded
1 c. Mozzarella cheese,
shredded

1 ½ c. Parmesan cheese,
grated (save ½ c. for top)
1 c. sour cream
2 Tbsp. butter, melted
1 small onion, chopped
1 (8 oz.) can mushrooms,
sliced
1 Tbsp. Worcestershire sauce
½ c. Kellogg's cornflake
crumbs
salt and pepper to taste

Saute onions, garlic and mushrooms in butter. Add soups, milk, chicken broth, sour cream, Worcestershire sauce, salt and pepper, stirring well. Add chicken and spaghetti until all mixed together, then add the cheeses and pour into a 9 x 13-inch baking dish.

Mix ½ cup Parmesan cheese with ½ cup cornflake crumbs and sprinkle on top of casserole. Bake in a 350° oven for 45 to 50 minutes. Let stand 15 minutes before serving.

Coffee-Braised Short Ribs With Ancho Chili

Sue Donham

(Serves 4 to 6)

2 Tbsp. olive oil
1 large onion, chopped
1 large jalapeno, seeded and
finely chopped
2 Tbsp. dark brown sugar
2 tsp. oregano
2 c. strong freshly brewed
coffee
1 Tbsp. tomato paste

5 lb. 1-inch thick short ribs
1 red bell pepper, seeded and
chopped
6 cloves garlic, chopped
1 ½ Tbsp. ancho chili powder
¼ tsp. ground cumin
14 oz. can diced tomatoes (in
juices)
fresh cilantro, chopped

Preheat oven to 300°. In a heavy, large ovenproof pot, heat oil over medium-high heat. Sprinkle ribs with salt and pepper. Working in batches, add ribs to the pot and cook until the ribs are browned on all sides (4 minutes per side), then transfer to a platter.

Add onion, jalapeno and bell pepper to the pot; reduce heat to medium. Cover and cook until the onion is tender (about 6 minutes). Stir in garlic and sauté for 1 minute. Add brown sugar, oregano, chili powder and cumin. Stir, then add coffee, tomato paste and diced tomatoes. Bring to a boil, scraping up the browned bits. Return ribs to the pot and bring to a boil.

Cover and bake until meat is very tender (about 1 hour and 45 minutes). Spoon fat from the surface of sauce; season with salt and pepper. Transfer ribs to a platter. Spoon sauce over and sprinkle with cilantro.

Can be prepared 1 day ahead. Just cool slightly, chill, uncovered, then cover and refrigerate. Reheat, covered, over medium heat.

Orange Cranberry Glazed Pork Tenderloin

Dee Judge

16 oz. can whole berry cranberry sauce	¼ tsp. ground allspice
1 tsp. grated orange rind	⅛ tsp. salt
⅔ c. fresh orange juice	⅛ tsp. ground cinnamon
2 tsp. balsamic vinegar	⅛ tsp. ground cloves
½ tsp. pepper	1 ½ lb. pork tenderloin
	1 ½ Tbsp. olive oil

Preheat oven to 425°. Bring first 9 ingredients to a boil over medium heat. Reduce heat and simmer, stirring occasionally, for 20 minutes. Remove from heat and set aside.

Brown pork in hot oil in a large nonstick skillet over medium-high heat for 3 minutes on each side or until golden brown. Place pork in a lightly greased shallow roasting pan. Bake for 25 to 30 minutes or until meat thermometer registers 155°, basting occasionally with some of the cranberry mixture.

Remove from oven; cover pork with foil and let stand for 5 minutes or until thermometer registers 160°. Slice pork and serve with cranberry mixture. Serves 8.

Chicken Stromboli

Rexene Goecker Wood

2 cans refrigerated crescent
  rolls
12 oz. can chicken
1 c. broccoli, cut into small
  pieces
1 c. cheese (more if needed)
2 tsp. dill weed

1 clove garlic, crushed
½ c. mayonnaise or salad
  dressing
½ c. red pepper, diced
¼ tsp. salt (optional)
egg whites, beaten
slivered almonds

Mix all ingredients together, except crescent rolls, egg whites and almonds. Place crescent rolls on cookie sheet end to end. Roll them into one long sheet. Slice across in about 8 pieces. A pizza cutter works well. Flatten the center area again.

Put the chicken mixture on the crescent rolls and fold the sides into the middle. Brush the top with egg whites. Sprinkle with slivered almonds on the top. Bake in a 350° oven for 25 to 28 minutes. Let set a few minutes before slicing.

Pacific Rim Tenderloin

Anna Broecker

(Serves 8)

4 Tbsp. soy suace
2 Tbsp. dry sherry or white
  wine
2 Tbsp. light brown sugar,
  pressed firmly
2 Tbsp. peanut oil
3 Tbsp. honey
1 tsp. garlic salt
1 tsp. ground cinnamon

1 c. chopped peanuts
2 lb. pork tenderloin
½ c. light brown sugar
¼ c. catsup
½ c. pineapple juice
⅓ c. cider vinegar
½ tsp. garlic powder
1 Tbsp. cornstarch
⅓ c. water

In a large Ziploc plastic bag, combine soy sauce, sherry, 2 tablespoons brown sugar, peanut oil, honey, garlic salt, cinnamon and peanuts. Add tenderloin; seal and refrigerate 8 hours, turning once.

Remove tenderloin (discard marinade) and grill 6 inches from coals for 30 to 35 minutes, turning often. Or bake at 350° for 40 to 50 minutes or to an internal temperature of 160°.

In a saucepan, combine remaining ingredients, except cornstarch and water. Bring to a boil and then add the cornstarch and water; stir to thicken. Slice thinly on the diagonal. Arrange 3 or 4 slices, then drizzle warm sauce down the center and garnish with chopped peanuts.

Pork Tenderloin

Elizabeth Smoth

1 pork tenderloin
1 c. crumbled bacon
3 cloves garlic, finely chopped

1 c. apple juice
3 Tbsp. water
2 Tbsp. cornstarch

Bake tenderloin at 350° for 30 to 40 minutes. Make sauce by using the rest of the ingredients. Slice pork and drizzle sauce over it. Serves 4 to 6.

FREE Recipe Symbol

Crabmeat Casserole

In Memory of Helen Johnson

6 potatoes, boiled with skins
   left on
5 Tbsp. butter
5 Tbsp. flour
½ c. green onions, chopped
⅔ c. chicken broth

1 c. grated cheese
2 sm. cans crabmeat
1 tsp. salt
2 c. half & half
1 c. Fritos

Cook potatoes in their skins until just tender; cool and peel. Slice about ¼ inch thick. Melt butter in saucepan. Add onions and cook slightly. Blend flour in butter until smooth. Gradually add milk and broth. Cook, stirring constantly until thick. Remove from heat. Line buttered casserole dish with sliced potatoes, crabmeat and cheese. Layer in that order, pouring cooked mixture over each layer. Top with Fritos and cook at 425° for about 20 minutes. A few shrimp layered with crabmeat is very good.

Beef and Noodle Casserole

Donna Tate

1 ½ lb. ground chuck
1 14 ½ oz. can diced
   tomatoes
1 can Ro-Tel
1 can tomato sauce
2 tsp. salt
2 tsp. sugar
2 cloves garlic, crushed

1 medium onion
1 c. sour cream
1 3 oz. cream cheese
2 c. grated cheese
1 pkg. linguine (from
   refrigerated section)
Mozzarella cheese

Saute onion. Add meat to skillet and cook until lightly browned. Drain off fat. Stir tomatoes and tomato sauce into the meat mixture. Add salt, sugar and garlic. Simmer until thickened. Cook noodles; drain well. Add sour cream and cream cheese to noodles. Lightly butter 3 qt. casserole dish. Pour small amount of meat sauce into dish. Cover with noodle mixture. Layer with grated cheese. Repeat layers, topping with sauce. Bake at 350° until bubbly about 40 minutes. top with mozzarella and heat until melted.

Cajun Shrimp Skewers

Sandy Scott

Marinade:

¾ c. vegetable oil
1 medium onion, finely
  chopped
2 Tbsp. Cajun seasoning
6 garlic cloves, minced

2 tsp. ground cumin
1 tsp minced fresh rosemary
1 tsp. minced fresh thyme
2 lbs. uncooked large shrimp,
  peeled and deveined

Cajun Butter:

1 c. butter, cubed
1 tsp. minced fresh basil
1 tsp. minced fresh tarragon

1 tsp. Cajun seasoning
½ tsp. garlic powder
3 drops hot pepper sauce

In a small bowl, combine the first seven ingredients. Place the shrimp in a large resealable plastic bag; add half of the marinade. Seal bag and turn to coat the shrimp; Chill for 1-2 hours. Save remaining marinade for basting later.

In a small saucepan, combine the Cajun butter ingredients; heat until butter is melted. Keep warm. Drain the shrimp and thread shrimp onto eight metal or soaked wooden skewers. Grill, uncovered, over medium heat 2-4 minutes on each side or until shrimp turn pink, basting once with reserved marinade. Serve with Cajun butter.

Lemon Turkey Breast

Martha Smitherman

1 4 lb. turkey breast
½ c. margarine, melted
¼ c. lemon juice

1 envelope Italian salad
  dressing mix

Place turkey breast into slow cooker. In a small bowl, combine margarine, lemon juice and dressing mix; pour over turkey. Cover and cook on low for 6 or more hours. Yield: 8 servings.

Parmesan Catfish

Linda Young

⅓ c. Parmesan cheese
⅔ c. Italian bread crumbs
4 farm-raised catfish fillets

margarine
salt and pepper to taste

Preheat oven to 350°. Rinse the catfish fillets with water and pat dry. Mix the Parmesan cheese and Italian bread crumbs together in a bowl. Dip the fillets in melted margarine to coat. Bread the fillets in cheese and crumb mixture, coating both sides well. Place the fillets in one layer in a lightly buttered glass dish. Do not crowd the fish. Any leftover breading may be sprinkled over the top of the fillets before baking. Bake fish 45 minutes or until well done and crunchy around the sides. Sprinkle with paprika and garnish with parsley, if desired.

Chicken Pie

Sandy Scott

1 chicken
1 ½ c. chicken broth
1 can cream of chicken soup
½ tsp. pepper

1 c. self-rising flour
1 stick margarine, melted
1 c. milk

Simmer chicken in salted water until tender, then debone. Cut up chicken and put in casserole dish. Combine soup and broth and pour over chicken.

Topping: Mix flour, pepper, milk and melted margarine. Pour over chicken. Bake 35 to 40 minutes at 425°.

Parmesan Chicken

Lisa Thompson

4 to 6 boneless, skinless
  chicken breasts
1 c. all-purpose flour
1 tsp. kosher salt
½ tsp. freshly ground black
  pepper
2 extra-large eggs

1 Tbsp. water
1 ¼ c. seasoned dry bread
  crumbs
½ c. freshly grated Parmesan,
  plus extra for serving
Unsalted butter
Olive oil

Pound the chicken breasts until they are ¼ inch thick. You can use either a meat mallet or a rolling pin. Combine the flour, salt and pepper on a dinner plate. On a second plate, beat the eggs with 1 Tablespoon of water. On a third plate, combine the bread crumbs and ½ cup grated Parmesan. Coat the chicken breasts on both sides with the flour mixture, then dip both sides into the egg mixture and dredge both sides in the bread-crumb mixture, pressing lightly.

Heat 1 Tablespoon of butter and 1 Tablespoon of olive oil in a large saute pan and cook 2 or 3 chicken breasts on medium-low heat for 2 to 3 minutes on each side, until cook through. Add more butter and oil an cook the rest of the chicken breasts. Yields 6 servings.

Oven Fried Chicken

Sandra VanZant

1 fryer, cut up
Salt and pepper
¼ c. Dijon-style mustard

¼ c. sour cream
1 c. cornflake crumbs or
   bread crumbs

Wash chicken and pat dry. Salt and pepper to taste. Spread with mustard, then sour cream. Coat with crumbs. Spread out on baking sheet. Bake in 350° oven for 1 hour.

Steamed Lobster

Teresa Guthrie

2 lobsters (1 ¼-1/½ lb. each)
2 c. water
1 tsp. sea salt

¼ lb. butter, melted
Lemon wedges

Put water and salt into a pot with a tight sealing lid and bring to a full boil. Set live lobsters in the pot, and cover. Cook lobsters 12 minutes. Add 5 minutes for each additional ½ pound of lobster. Remove cover (being careful of the steam) and remove lobsters to heated plates. Nut crackers will be needed to crack the shells. Serve immediately with warm melted butter and lemon wedges.

FREE Recipe Symbol

Super Easy Steak and Gravy

Grace Hollaman

1 round steak
1 can cream of mushroom
   soup

1 pkg. Lipton onion soup mix

In greased baking dish put round steak. Sprinkle onion soup mix over steak. Cover with cream of mushroom soup. Cover with foil and bake at 350° for 45 minutes. Do not peak.

Chicken Enchiladas

Helen Johnson

4 chicken breasts (boiled and
  deboned)
flour tortillas
1 large salsa

2 c. Cheddar cheese
  (shredded)
1 can cream of mushroom
  soup
1 (16 oz.) sour cream

Mix salsa with chicken. Fill tortilla with chicken mixture. Place filled tortillas in casserole dish. Mix soup and sour cream. Pour mixture over tortillas. Sprinkle cheese on top and bake at 350° until cheese is melted and mixture is bubbly.

Spaghetti and Oysters

Joyce Goode

1 stick butter
½ c. parsley
¼ c. flour
1 c. chopped green onions
1 qt. oyster water

½ oz. Lea & Perrins sauce
1 tsp. Accent
2 doz. small oysters
salt and pepper to taste
1 lb. spaghetti, cooked

Melt butter. Blend in flour and cook until foam appears. Do not brown. Next, boil the oysters in oyster water until edges of oysters curl. Add boiling water from oysters to the flour and stir rapidly over medium heat. Cook ten minutes. Add parsley and green onions, Lea and Perrins Sauce, accent and seasonings. Cook 15 minutes over low heat.

Jambalaya

Judy Shaker

2 onions, chopped
4 Tbsp. butter
1 can tomatoes
½ can tomato paste
2 cloves garlic, chopped
2 pieces celery, chopped
¼ green pepper, chopped

1 tsp. parsley
½ tsp. thyme
3 cloves, chopped
1 lb. boiled ham, diced
2 lbs. peeled, boiled shrimp
3 c. cooked rice
salt, pepper, cayenne to taste

Saute onions in butter five minutes. Add tomatoes, tomato paste, and cook five minutes, stirring. Add all seasoning, chopped very fine. Cook ½ hour, stirring frequently. Stir in ham and cook for about 5 minutes longer. Add shrimp and continue cooking another 5 minutes. Stir in cooked rice and season. Simmer for about ½ hour, stirring frequently.

Chicken Gumbo

Pat Martin

1 small stewing hen	2 Tbsp. chopped parsley
2 Tbsp. flour	2 c. chicken stock or water
2 chopped onions	1 pinch thyme
1 c. celery	2 bay leaves
2 c. okra	3 Tbsp. shortening
2 c. tomatoes	1 tsp. celery salt

Cut chicken into serving portions. Dredge lightly in flour. Saute in melted shortening until brown. Add onions and celery, cooking until soft. Add all other ingredients except the okra. Cook until the chicken is tender. Add okra and cook an additional 15 minutes. Salt and pepper to taste. Serve over rice.

Shrimp Etouffee

Helen Barton

1 Tbsp. butter	1 tsp. chopped parsley
1 c. tiny shrimp	Salt and pepper to taste
¼ tsp. chopped garlic	

Melt butter in saucepan. Add the small shrimp (size 50-60 per lb.) Stir in minced garlic, salt and pepper and cook over medium heat for about 10 minutes. Add chopped parsley. Serve with butter rice. Serves 2.

Fried Fantail Shrimp In Beer Batter

Joan Crawford

1 c. sifted flour	1 tsp. baking powder
½ tsp. sugar	1 beaten egg
½ tsp. salt	1 c. beer
Dash pepper	2 lb. fresh shrimp
Dash nutmeg	Cooking oil for frying

Mix all ingredients, (except the shrimp) to make the batter. Peel shell from shrimp, leaving the last section and tail intact. Cut almost through shrimp at the center back without cutting ends.

Dry shrimp and dip into beer batter. Fry in deep, hot fat until golden brown. Drain and serve at once.

Poppy Seed Chicken

Marian Gibson

6 chicken breasts
1 c. sour cream
2 cans cream of chicken soup

1 stack Ritz crackers
½ stick butter (margarine)
1 Tbsp. poppy seed

Boil chicken and debone. Place layer of chicken in bottom of baking dish. Mix sour cream and soup; pour ½ of mixture on top of chicken. Crush crackers. Melt butter and mix both with poppy seed. Place ½ of this over sour cream mixture. Add another layer of chicken, soup mixture and crumbs. Bake at 350° until mixture boils, about 25 minutes.

Smothered Steak

Peggy Hardwick

1 (2 ½ lb.) boneless round
  steak, cut into serving
  pieces, seasoned
salt and pepper to taste
¼ c. canola oil
1 tsp. garlic salt

1 Tbsp. Worcestershire sauce
dash of hot sauce
2 Tbsp. red wine vinegar
2 c. plus 2 Tbsp. water
4 green pepper rings or more
  if you like

Prep Time: 50 to 60 minutes. Serves: 6 to 8.

Sprinkle steak with salt and pepper; dredge in flour. Heat oil in a large skillet; brown meat on both sides.

Combine 3 tablespoons flour, garlic salt, Worcestershire sauce, hot sauce, wine vinegar and 2 tablespoons water; stir until smooth. Add remaining water; stir until blended.

Pour mixture over steak and top with green pepper rings. Cover and cook over low heat 50 to 60 minutes or until tender. Add water as it cooks to keep meat from sticking and make enough gravy to serve over rice or potatoes.

Fresh Garland Graphics

VEGETABLES

Recipe Format 14

*O*VEN FRIES

2 Russet potatoes
¼ c. extra virgin olive oil
¾ tsp. kosher salt

2 Tbsp. chopped parsley
leaves
¼ c. freshly grated
Parmigiana-Reggiano

Preheat oven to 425°. Preheat a baking sheet in hot oven for at least 5 minutes.

Cut potatoes in ½ lengthwise. Cut halves lengthwise into fourths to make 16 big fat wedges. While the baking sheet is heating, toss the potatoes with the olive oil and salt in a large bowl. Then dump the potatoes out onto a baking sheet, spreading to a single layer.

Roast for 30 to 35 minutes, shaking the pan every now and then, until the potatoes are cooked through, brown and crispy. Toss the fries in a big bowl with the parsley and cheese.

Valerie Wing

*I*TALIAN GREEN BEANS

1 lb. Italian green beans
olive oil
1 clove garlic

¼ tsp. oregano
salt and pepper to taste

Cook beans until partially tender; drain and saute in olive oil, 1 clove garlic and oregano. Add salt and pepper. Cook until tender.

Kenny Clark

Non-Continued Recipe Option without fillers

$\mathcal{S}$PINACH AND RICOTTA QUICHE

Crust:
8 oz. flour	1 egg
4 oz. butter (room temperature)	salt

Mix the flour, butter, egg and a pinch of salt. Place in refrigerator for 30 minutes. Roll out dough to a thin and round shape.

Line a 9-inch pie pan with parchment paper. Place dough into pan and set aside. Don't throw away extra dough, you may want to cover the quiche.

Filling:
18 oz. frozen spinach	salt and pepper
8 oz. Ricotta cheese (I prefer whole milk Ricotta)	olive oil
1 garlic clove	1 c. grated Parmesan cheese

Cook spinach as directed; drain and squeeze out all the water and chop.

In a frying pan, add oil and saute garlic and spinach on medium heat for 5 to 7 minutes. Salt and pepper to taste.

Cool spinach, then add Ricotta and Parmesan cheeses. Mix well. Add the mixture to the dough and place in 350° oven. Bake for 20 minutes.

If you have extra dough, roll out and cover the mixture.

Royce Rollins

$\mathcal{R}$ANCH POTATOES

1 (5 lb.) bag potatoes	1 bag real bacon bits
1 large bottle Ranch dressing	salt and pepper
1 small container sour cream	Cajun seasoning (optional)
1 lb. bag shredded cheese	

Preheat oven to 400°. Cube potatoes in large baking dish sprayed with Pam and seasoned with salt, pepper and Cajun seasoning. Use ½ of Ranch dressing by pouring over potatoes. Add just enough water to cover bottom of pan. This keeps potatoes from drying out.

Stir all other ingredients together, except sour cream and Ranch dressing. Bake at 400° for about an hour and 15 minutes or until potatoes are soft. Add remaining Ranch. Stir good and layer sour cream on top and top with cheese and bacon bits.

Summer Thorne

HOLIDAY YAM BAKE

1 (40 oz.) can yams
1 (8 ½ oz.) can crushed
  pineapple and juice or
raisins
2 Tbsp. light brown sugar

2 Tbsp. butter or margarine,
  melted
3 Tbsp. chopped pecans
¾ c. miniature
  marshmallows

Drain yams; mash well. Drain pineapple; reserve juice. Add juice to yams. Add sugar and butter; beat well. Stir in pineapple and pecans. Coat inside of 1 ½-quart casserole with Pam. Spoon in mixture. Bake for 20 minutes at 350°. Sprinkle with marshmallows. Bake for 10 minutes longer. Serves 8.

John Johnson

FRIED CABBAGE

4 bacon slices
1 large head fresh cabbage,
  coarsely chopped

1 tsp. salt
1 tsp. black pepper

Cook bacon in a large skillet for 10 minutes or until crisp. Remove bacon, and drain on paper towels, reserving 1 tablespoon drippings in skillet. Add cabbage to hot drippings in skillet; sprinkle with salt and pepper. Saute cabbage over medium-high heat for 10 to 12 minutes or until tender. Crumble bacon and sprinkle over cooked cabbage.

Jennifer Moree

FRIED CORN ON THE COB

1 pkg. niblet corn on the cob
  (frozen)

flour
buttermilk

Dredge corn in buttermilk and flour. Heat oil and deep fry until golden brown.

Jennifer Moree

*E*GGPLANT CASSEROLE

1 large eggplant, peeled and
   sliced.
butter milk
egg
flour
salt and pepper

2 to 3 c. shredded Cheddar
   cheese or red rind
fresh salsa or salsa in a jar
1 large bag of Doritos,
   crushed

Soak eggplant in buttermilk and egg mixture. Dredge in flour, salt and pepper mixture. Deep fry then place on paper towel to soak up the grease. Cut eggplant into cubes. In a buttered baking dish, layer as follows, salsa, chips, cheese, and fried eggplant. Repeat layers. Bake at 325°until bubby. Serve warm

Carolyn Kennedy

*S*QUASH FRITTERS

2 c. cooked squash
¼ c. chopped onion
1 egg, beaten

salt and pepper to taste
Cracker crumbs, enough to
   be able to form into patties.

Combine all ingredients and mix well. Shape and form patties. Fry in oil, turn to brown on both sides.

Carolyn Bryant

*G*REEN BEAN BUNDLES

2 or 3 c. whole green beans
   (drained)
1 lb. bacon

1 c. brown sugar
½ c. vinegar
salt and pepper to taste

Drain green beans and put into bowl. Cut bacon slices in half and wrap around bundles of beans. I usually put 7 or 8 beans per bundle. Place the bundles in a 9x13 casserole dish. Combine brown sugar, vinegar, and salt and pepper. Heat in saucepan then pour over the bundles. Cook on 350° to 375° for 30 minutes or until bacon is cooked brown.

Janice Duncan

$\mathcal{S}$TUFFED RIPE TOMATOES

6 or 8 ripe red tomatoes
½ skillet corn bread (as you
usually prepare)
1 onion chopped to be cooked
in with corn bread mix

3 Tbsp. sugar
salt and pepper to taste
3 slices of bacon
½ to 1 c. milk to moisten
mixture

Cut the tops off tomatoes--vine side. Scoop out the pulp from the tomatoes and place in mixing bowl. Into this mix, add the corn bread, sugar and salt and pepper. Place this mixture into the scooped-out tomatoes. Cut the bacon slices into pieces and place on top of tomatoes. Place in 9x13 casserole dish and bake in 375° oven for 30 to 45 minutes or until bacon is crisp.

Janice Duncan

$\mathcal{E}$GGPLANT CASSEROLE

1 large or 2 small eggplants
2 eggs beaten
1 tsp. sugar
1 c. grated cheese (Cheddar)
1 c. crackers crumbs

½ stick of butter
½ c. chopped celery
1 c. chopped onions
1 can cream of mushroom
soup

Peel and chop eggplant and boil until done.
Saute onions and celery in 1 tablespoon of butter. Drain eggplant and add onion and celery, add sugar, eggs, cheese soup and ½ cup cracker crumbs, melt butter and pour over top, then sprinkle the other half of crumbs on top. Cook at 350° for 30 minutes.

Diane Dunaway

$\mathcal{C}$ORN AND RICE CASSEROLE

2 cans sweet corn
2 small packs yellow rice
1 can cream of mushroom
soup

16 oz. Velveeta cheese
½ c. milk

Cook yellow rice according direction on back of package. In a 9x13 pan place cooked rice, corn, and cream of mushroom and mix together. Then in a separate bowl cut Velveeta cheese and milk and microwave until melted. Then, add the cheese to the 9x13 pan and mix all ingredient together. Bake at 350° for 30 to 45 minutes.

Stephanie Draughn, Petal Branch

_M_ASHED POTATOES

1 pkg. Hidden Valley,
original Ranch Dressing
mix

4 c. unsalted mashed
potatoes, with or without
skins

Add dressing mix to potatoes; stir well. Serve with butter.

Sandy Vann

_M_ASHED POTATO CASSEROLE

10 medium size potatoes,
peeled
1 c. sour cream
1 c. cottage cheese
1 Tbsp. grated onion

½ c. butter
¼ tsp. pepper
1 tsp. salt
¼ c. grated Parmesan cheese

Boil potatoes in salted water until tender. Mash. While still hot, add the sour cream, cottage cheese, onion, butter, pepper and salt. Mix well.

Place in a casserole. Sprinkle Parmesan on top. Bake in a 325° oven for 30 minutes. Serves 8-10.

Sandy Vann

_S_QUASH DRESSING

2 c. cooked squash
2 c. cooked cornbread
½ chopped onion
2 eggs

1 can cream of chicken soup
stick of margarine, melted
salt & pepper to taste

Preheat oven to 375°. Spray a 2 ½ quart casserole with no stick cooking spray and set aside. In a large bowl, combine all ingredients until thoroughly mixed and pour into prepared dish. Bake for 30-40 minutes.

Jennifer H. Thompson

_B_ACON WRAPPED GREEN BEANS

6 cans whole green beans
1 pkg. of bacon

brown sugar
½ c. margarine

Preheat oven on 375°. Drain beans. Get a bundle of beans (around 8). Wrap ½ slice of bacon around each bundle. Lay each bundle wrap side down in a baking pan. Do not overlap. Melt margarine. Pour over bean bundles. Put ½ teaspoon brown sugar on each bundle. Bake until bacon is done.

Dawn Rowell

$\mathcal{O}$VEN ROASTED SWEET POTATOES AND ONIONS

4 medium sweet potatoes,
  peeled and cut into 2 inch
  pieces
2 medium Vidalia onions
  sliced

2 Tbsp. extra virgin olive oil
¾ tsp. garlic-pepper blend
½ tsp. salt

Combine all ingredients in a 9X13 inch baking dish, tossing to coat. Bake in 425° oven 35 minutes or until tender, stir occasionally.

Sandy Vann

$\mathcal{C}$ORN PUDDING

6 to 8 ears of corn
3 eggs
½ c. whipping cream
½ c. milk
½ c. white Cheddar

¼ tsp. cayenne pepper
2 Tbsp. melted butter
2 Tbsp. sugar
1 Tbsp. self-rising flour
1 tsp. salt

Cut corn off the cob. Beat eggs. Add all ingredients together. Pour into a buttered 1 quart casserole dish. Bake at 350° for 45 minutes to 1 hour.
Can substitute low-fat ingredients.
Can use 2 frozen sleeves of corn and add more self-rising flour or cracker crumbs.

Donna McComb

$\mathcal{A}$SPARAGUS CASSEROLE

2 cans asparagus
4 boiled eggs, chopped
1 can cream of mushroom
  soup
approximately 3 c. grated
  cheese

salt
pepper
crackers or potato chips,
  crushed

In casserole dish put a layer of asparagus, egg and cheese, sprinkle salt and pepper, I do this before the cheese, repeat for second layer. Combine small amount of asparagus juice with mushroom soup; pour over top of layers. With knife, work soup mixture down into layers. Top with more chips or crackers. Bake at 350° until mixture is bubbly and cheese is melted.

Tina Martin

ITALIAN ZUCCHINI CASSEROLE

2-3 lb. zucchini
½ c. chopped onion
½ c. chopped green pepper
4 Tbsp. margarine
1 pkg. spaghetti sauce mix

½ c. shredded Cheddar
cheese
1 4 oz. can mushrooms
1 6 oz. can tomato paste
1 c. water
Grated Parmesan cheese

Slice zucchini into ½ inch pieces and drop into boiling water. Cook 4-5 minutes and drain. Place zucchini in casserole dish. Saute onion and green pepper in margarine. Add sauce mix, Cheddar cheese, mushrooms, tomato paste, and water. Mix well and pour over zucchini. Sprinkle top with Parmesan cheese. Bake 25-30 minutes at 350° Let stand 10 minutes before serving.

Sandy Vann

STUFFED BAKED EGGPLANT

2 firm eggplants
1 stick butter
1 Tbsp. chopped parsley
4 Tbsp. shallots, chopped
very fine
Salt and pepper to taste

1 c. lump crabmeat
1 c. cooked shrimp
1 c. finely grated Parmesan
cheese
¼ c. bread crumbs

Cut the eggplants in half and place in the oven in a pan that has about a cup of water in the bottom to steam the eggplant. Bake until tender; scoop out the center of the eggplant, leaving the shell for stuffing. Brown shallots and parsley in butter over low heat. Add shrimp, crabmeat, and the pulp of the eggplant. Season with salt and pepper.
Stir together and cook for five minutes. Fill the shells. Then sprinkle with cheese and bread crumbs. Bake 350° until browned.

Joey Temples, Carriere Branch

STUFFED EGGPLANT

8 oz. ham
8 oz. lump Crab meat
1 onion
1 bell pepper
2 stalks celery

2 cloves of garlic
1 c. cracker crumbs
2 eggplant
2 oz. Parmesan cheese
Salt and pepper

Chop onion, bell pepper, celery, garlic, and ham. Saute for 10 minutes. Cut eggplant into quarters and boil for 30 minutes. Scoop out the eggplant and blend it with the seasonings. Fold in the cracker crumbs, cheese, and crab meat. Salt and pepper to taste. Place dressing back into eggplant shells. Sprinkle with more cheese and crumbs. Bake 350° until brown.

Joey Temples, Carriere Branch

VEGETABLES

HIDDEN VALLEY RANCH POTOTOES

6 medium red potatoes or
  new potatoes
1 ½ stick margarine melted

1 pkg. Hidden Valley Ranch
  dressing mix

Slice potatoes. Place in dish. Mix margarine and dressing mix together. Pour over potatoes. Cook covered 350° for 45 minutes or until done.

Donna Byrd

AUNT GUSSIE'S SQUASH CASSEROLE

2 lbs. squash, cooked until
  done, drained, and mashed
1 stick margarine, melted
3 eggs, beaten
1 c. cracker crumbs

1 Tbsp. sugar
Salt to taste
1 c. cheese
½ c milk
Chopped onion (preference)

Add all ingredients and stir. Bake at 350° for one hour or until done.

Dawn Rowell
Aunt Gussie Rowley

CABBAGE CASSEROLE

1 head cabbage shredded
1 large onion
½ stick butter
½ small block of Velveeta
  cheese

1 can cream of mushroom
  soup
bread crumbs

Boil cut up cabbage 10 minutes in salted water. Saute onions in butter. Mix melted cheese, soup and onions. Drain cabbage and pour in 13x9 baking dish. Pour mixture over cabbage and lightly top with bread crumbs. Bake at 325° for 30 minutes.

Melanie Stoll

Non-Continued Recipe Option
without fillers

5000409

$\mathcal{S}$HOE PEG CORN CASSEROLE

½ c. chopped celery
½ c. chopped green pepper
½ c. chopped onion
1 can French cut beans
  (drained)
¾ c. grated cheese

1 can cream of mushroom
  soup
1 c. sour cream
1 stick butter
1 stack of Ritz crackers

Saute celery, onions and peppers in a little oil. Then mix first 8 ingredients and pour in 8 ½ x 11 casserole dish. Crush Ritz crackers and mix with melted butter. Cover top of casserole with cracker mixture. Bake at 350° until bubbly. About 45 minutes.

Melanie Stoll

$\mathcal{Y}$AM PATTIES

1 stick butter
1 c. sugar
½ c. water

1 tsp. vanilla
1 pkg. round yam patties

Mix ingredients in pot over burner until sugar dissolves. Pour over yams and bake until hot.

Melanie Stoll

$\mathcal{T}$WICE BAKED POTATOES

4 baked potatoes, cut in half,
  lengthwise
1 c. shredded Cheddar cheese
⅓ c. milk
½ tsp. salt

dash of pepper
¼ c. sliced green onions
garlic powder to taste
  (optional)
Hormel bacon bits

Scoop out center of potatoes and mash. Add shredded cheese, milk, salt and pepper. Stir in sliced green onions and garlic powder. Spoon into shells and top with bacon bits first then top with extra shredded cheese. Bake at 350° for 20 to 25 minutes.

Dianne Barber

*B*ACON POTATO SALAD

6 to 8 medium potatoes
(about 3 lbs.) peeled and
cut into 1-inch cubes
½ of real bacon bits
2 Tbsp. diced pimiento,
drained

¾ tsp. salt
¼ tsp. pepper
½ c. mayonnaise
½ c. sour cream

Cook potatoes in boiling water to cover in a Dutch Oven over medium heat 15 to 18 minutes or until done. Drain and let cool slightly.
Place potatoes in a large bowl. Add bacon bits, and next 3 ingredients. Stir together mayonnaise and sour cream until blended. Pour over potato mixture, tossing gently to coat. Cover and chill at least 1 hour.

Kim Hall

*B*ROCCOLI RICE CASSEROLE

1 stick butter, melted
1 small onion, chopped
1 can cream of chicken soup
16 oz. Cheez Whiz

10 to 16 oz. broccoli
pieces(fresh) or 2 pkgs.
frozen (cooked)
1 ½ c. cooked rice

Melt butter and saute onion. Add soup and cheese to onions. After mixture melts, add cooked
broccoli and rice. Mix and place in casserole dish. Bake at 350° for 30 minutes.

Dianne Barber

*S*QUASH CASSEROLE

3 c. cooked squash
1 c. Ritz crackers
1 c. Cheddar cheese (mild)
1 can cream of chicken soup

1 small onion
1 tsp. salt
½ tsp. pepper
1 egg

Drain squash. Crumble crackers and grated cheese. Reserve ½ of the crackers and cheese for topping. Place squash, ½ of cheese, ½ of crackers, onion (chopped), and other ingredients in 3 quart casserole. Top with remaining cheese and crackers. Bake at 325° for 45 minutes. Serve 6.

Dianne Barber

SQUASH DRESSING

2 c. yellow squash, sliced
1 onion, chopped
1 c. water
2 c. cornbread crumbs
2 eggs

1 can (10-¾-oz) cream of
    chicken soup, undiluted
¼ c. oleo, melted
¼ tsp. pepper
Cheddar cheese, grated

Combine squash, onion and water in sauce pan. Cover and cook until tender. Drain and mash. Combine with remaining ingredients except cheese and spoon into greased casserole. Top with grated Cheddar cheese. Bake at 350° for 25 minutes or until thoroughly heated. Makes 4-6 servings.

Dianne Barber

BOSTON BAKED BEANS

2 lb. pea beans
1 tsp. baking soda
½ lb. salt pork
8 Tbsp. sugar

⅔ c. molasses
2 tsp. dry mustard
½ tsp. pepper

Soak beans overnight. In morning, parboil them for 10 minutes with a teaspoon of baking soda, then run cold water through the beans in a colander. Dice rind of salt pork in 1-inch squares; divide in half. Put half in 2-quart bean pot (bottom). Put beans in pot. Put rest of pork on top. Mix other ingredients with hot water. Pour over beans. Bake in 300° oven for 6 hours. Add more water when needed. Uncover for last half hour.

Bonnie Betts

CHEESY APPLES

1 (16 oz.) can Comstock
    apples (undrained)
½ c. butter
½ c. sugar

¾ c. flour
8 oz. Velveeta cheese, cubed
¼ c. milk

Place apples in a greased 1 ½-quart casserole dish. Combine remaining ingredients in a saucepan. Cook and stir over medium heat until cheese melts and all is well blended. Spread over apples. Bake, uncovered, at 350° for 30 to 40 minutes or until top is brown.

Lisa Thomas

$\mathcal{S}$UNDAY APRICOT CASSEROLE

butter
2 (15 oz.) cans apricots (in
light syrup)

brown sugar
Ritz crackers

Butter 2 oblong casserole dishes. Layer apricots and syrup in dishes. Cover completely and cover with thick layer of brown sugar. Cover with crushed Ritz crackers (at least 2 sleeves). Dot top heavily with butter. Bake at 300° for 1 hour. Serve with meat and vegetable.

Jan Lancaster

$\mathcal{A}$RTICHOKE HEARTS WRAPPED IN BACON

1 (12 oz.) jar marinated
artichoke heart quarters
9 slices center-cut bacon,
halved

Kraft Parmesan cheese
(optional)

Preheat oven to 425°. Line baking sheet with foil. Drain artichoke heart quarters; reserve liquid. Wrap artichoke heart quarters with half slice of bacon; secure with toothpick.

Place on baking sheet and drizzle with reserved liquid. Sprinkle with cheese. Bake in oven for 10 to 15 minutes or until lightly browned. Serve warm.

Mrs. Judy Seely

$\mathcal{S}$USAN'S BROCCOLI

2 (10 oz.) pkg. chopped
broccoli (cook and drain)
½ c. mayo
2 eggs, beaten
1 can cream of mushroom
soup

1 tsp. salt
1 tsp. pepper
1 c. grated cheese
⅔ c. chopped onion

Place broccoli in greased casserole; cover with mixed remaining ingredients. Bake at 350° for approximately 30 minutes. If desired, top with additional cheese before baking.

Judy (Day) Burgess

CABBAGE CASSEROLE

1 large cabbage, cut and
steamed
3 tsp. olive oil
1 medium onion, chopped
3 toes garlic, chopped
3 to 4 green onions, chopped

1 tsp. salt
½ tsp. pepper
½ c. Italian bread crumbs
½ c. Romano cheese
2 eggs, beaten
3 Tbsp. butter

Heat oil in saucepan and saute onion, green onions and garlic. Add steamed cabbage, salt, pepper and egg. Add ½ of cheese and crumbs. Spoon into a buttered casserole dish. Top with remaining bread crumbs and cheese. Dot with butter. Bake at 350°.

Mary Reaney-Gates

CARROT SOUFFLÉ

1 ¾ lb. peeled carrots
¾ c. sugar
1 ½ tsp. baking powder
1 ½ tsp. vanilla
2 Tbsp. flour

3 eggs (beat with electric
mixer)
1 stick oleo
powdered sugar

Steam or boil carrots until very soft. Drain well. Put in large mixer bowl. When carrots are warm, add sugar, baking powder and vanilla. Beat with mixer until smooth. Add flour and mix well. Add whipped eggs and beat well. Add oleo and blend well.

Pour mixture in 2-quart dish. Bake at 350° for 1 hour. Sprinkle lightly with sugar before serving. Serves 8 to 10.

Brittany Hemphill

CORN CASSEROLE

2 cans creamed corn
¾ c. Jiffy cornbread mix
¼ c. oil
1 can green chiles

¾ c. sharp grated cheese
(Cheddar)
2 eggs, beaten
¾ tsp. garlic salt

Mix together the ingredients and bake at 350° for approximately 45 minutes.

Shirley Cole Johnson

$\mathcal{G}$ENUINE CREAMED CORN

2 (10 oz.) pkg. frozen kernel
  corn
1 c. whipping cream
1 c. milk
½ tsp. salt

2 Tbsp. sugar
2 Tbsp. melted butter
2 Tbsp. flour
fresh grated Parmesan
  cheese

Combine frozen corn, whipping cream, milk, salt and sugar in a saucepan and bring to a boil, stirring often. Reduce heat and simmer 5 minutes. Increase heat again until mixture reaches a low boil. Quickly blend the flour into the melted butter and stir into the corn mixture. Remove from heat.

Place corn in a shallow casserole dish and sprinkle with freshly grated Parmesan cheese. Place under broiler until evenly browned.

Marilyn Long

$\mathcal{S}$CALLOPED CORN AND TOMATOES

1 can creamed corn
1 (No. 2) can tomatoes
1 c. cracker crumbs
2 tsp. salt
¼ tsp. pepper
¼ tsp. paprika

2 Tbsp. sugar
2 eggs, beaten
¼ lb. grated Cheddar cheese
3 Tbsp. butter, melted
½ c. milk (optional)

Combine corn and tomatoes; mix thoroughly. Add cracker crumbs, salt, pepper, paprika and sugar and mix well. Add eggs, cheese, butter and milk if mixture is too thick. Pour into casserole dish and bake at 350° for 45 minutes.

This is a great side for grilled meats.

Karen Miller

$\mathcal{P}$INEAPPLE DRESSING

1 (20 oz.) can crushed
  pineapple, drained
½ c. margarine
1 c. sugar

5 slices bread crumbs (use
  food processor or blender)
4 eggs

Cream sugar and margarine. Add beaten eggs and drained pineapple. Mix well. Add bread crumbs. Bake at 350° until brown. I always double this recipe. Takes about 1 hour to brown.

Nellanne Davis

$\mathcal{A}$U GRATIN POTATOES

2 lb. bag frozen hash browns, shredded	8 oz. grated Cheddar cheese (may use white Vermont Cheddar)
2 cans cream of potato soup	
1 c. sour cream	½ medium red onion, chopped (optional)
1 c. milk	garlic powder and pepper to taste

Mix ingredients in large bowl. Put potatoes in greased 9 x 13 pan. Pour ingredients over it and mix well. Bake at 325° for 2 hours (1 hour, covered and 1 hour, uncovered).

Bonnie Siebert

$\mathcal{G}$OURMET BAKED POTATOES

1 baking potato	butter
2 to 3 thin slices white onion	sour cream (if desired)
1 strip bacon	salt
cooking oil	pepper

Prepare each ingredient for each person served.

Scrub potato with cold water and dry it. Lightly grease skin with oil. Split potato lengthwise. Place onion slices between the two halves. Put halves back together and wrap bacon strip around them to hold halves in place. Lay strip on bottom.

Wrap whole potatoes in foil. Place on baking sheet. Bake at 350° for 1 ½ hours or until soft.

Serve hot. Split and add salt, pepper, butter and sour cream to taste. One whole potato equals one serving.

Sue Dabbs

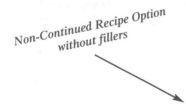

Non-Continued Recipe Option
without fillers